TRUE COLORS

An EFL Course for Real Communication

3

Jay Maurer
Irene E. Schoenberg

Joan Saslow

Series Director

Longman

True Colors: An EFL Course for Real Communication 3

Pearson Education, 10 Bank Street, White Plains, NY 10606

Editorial director: Allen Ascher
Development editor: Jessica Miller
Director of design and production: Rhea Banker
Production manager: Marie McNamara
Managing editor: Linda Moser
Senior production editor: Christine Cervoni
Associate production editor: Christine Lauricella
Photo research: Aerin Csigay
Cover design: Rhea Banker
Text design: Word & Image Design
Text composition: Word & Image Design
Manufacturing supervisor: Edie Pullman
Text art: Pierre Berthiaume, Jocelyne Bouchard, Andrée Chevrier, Patrick Fitzgerald,
    Brian Hughes, Stephen MacEachern, Jock MacRae, John Mantha, Paul McCusker,
    Dave McKay, Dusan Petricic, Stephen Quinlan, Philip Scheuer, Margot Thompson
Photo credits: Gilbert Duclos; page 9, Photofest; page 31, Printed by permission of the
    Norman Rockwell Family Trust Copyright © 1930 the Norman Rockwell Family Trust.
    © The Curtis Publishing Company; page 90, photo 1, © The Stock Market/Thomas H. Ives;
    page 90, photo 2, © The Stock Market/Bill Wassman, 1993; page 90, photo 3, © The Stock
    Market/Dilip Mehta, 1993; page 90, photo 4, © The Stock Market/David Pollack, 1990;
    page 91, © The Stock Market/David L. Brown, 1992; page 115, © AP/ Wide World Photos

Library of Congress Cataloging-in-Publication Data

Maurer, Jay.
    True colors: an EFL course for real communication/Jay Maurer; Irene E. Schoenberg;
    Joan Saslow, series director
        p. cm.
    1. English language—Textbooks for foreign speakers.
2. Communication.   I. Schoenberg, Irene.   II. Saslow, Joan M.   III. Title.

PE1128.M3548   1998

428.2'4—dc21   97-12071
                                                              CIP

ISBN: 0-201-18788-4

        5 6 7 8 9 10—WC—03 02 01

Contents

Scope and Sequence of Specific Content and Skills

UNIT	Social Language	Grammar and Pronunciation	Listening	Reading
1 I've been looking forward to this movie. page 2	How to: • make polite requests • offer a favor • agree to requests • ask someone to repeat a request • ask for advice • make a suggestion	Grammar: • the present perfect continuous	Types: • a phone conversation • movie reviews Comprehension Skills: • factual recall • listening between the lines	Type: • a photo story Comprehension Skill: • understanding meaning from context
2 When was Pluto discovered? page 14	How to: • ask about rules • express certainty • ask for and give an opinion	Grammar: • the passive voice Pronunciation: • stress and meaning	Types: • a photo story • a weather report Comprehension Skills: • factual recall • focus attention	Type: • a news article Comprehension Skill: • inference and interpretation
3 This lunch might end up costing me an arm and a leg. page 26	How to: • ask and tell about an occupation • ask for and give an opinion • confirm location	Grammar: • *may* and *might* • tag questions	Types: • a radio program • a conversation Comprehension Skills: • factual recall • listening between the lines	Type: • a photo story Comprehension Skill: • inference and interpretation
4 I don't make as much money as I used to. page 38	How to: • confirm information • emphasize an opinion • express surprise at a change	Grammar: • comparisons with *as* • *used to* Pronunciation: • *didn't you, wouldn't you, don't you, can't you* linkage	Types: • a photo story • a conversation with a realtor Comprehension Skills: • understanding meaning from context • focus attention	Type: • a newspaper article Comprehension Skill: • understanding grammar from context
5 If I were you, I'd speak to Glen first. page 50	How to: • respond to anger • persuade someone not to act impulsively • empathize • suggest a course of action • persuade someone not to do something	Grammar: • the present unreal conditional	Types: • a radio show • phone conversations Comprehension Skills: • understanding meaning from context • determine context • focus attention	Type: • a photo story Comprehension Skill: • inference and interpretation
Review of Units 1-5 page 62				
6 I wonder if she forgot about the party. page 72	How to: • ask about someone's identity • offer an explanation • ask for and make a suggestion • offer and accept help • reassure someone	Grammar: • embedded questions Pronunciation: • prefixes	Types: • a photo story • a conversation Comprehension Skills: • understanding meaning from context • focus attention	Type: • a magazine article Comprehension Skill: • inference and interpretation
7 We must be close to the top by now. page 84	How to: • state possibilities • express irritation • express obligations • draw conclusions • give surprising information • express surprise	Grammar: • *must, might,* and *can't* • *must* and *should*	Type: • a conversation Comprehension Skill: • listening between the lines	Type: • a photo story Comprehension Skill: • understanding meaning from context
8 She's the kind of person who's always there for you. page 96	How to: • talk about job possibilities • describe a person's qualities	Grammar: • adjective clauses Pronunciation: • *that*–stressed and unstressed	Types: • a photo story • a phone conversation Comprehension Skills: • understanding meaning from context • determine context • focus attention	Type: • a magazine article Comprehension Skill: • summarizing
9 Did you think you would live to be a hundred? page 108	How to: • talk about intention • express concern for someone • empathize • cancel a date and apologize • make another date	Grammar: • *was going to* and *would* + base form	Types: • a conversation • a radio program Comprehension Skills: • understanding grammar from context • focus attention	Type: • a photo story Comprehension Skill: • understanding meaning from context
10 He wants you to call him. He says it's important. page 120	How to: • give a message • express strong agreement • ask for a promise • agree to a promise	Grammar: • infinitives • verb forms for emphasis Pronunciation: • stress for contradiction	Types: • a photo story • a conversation Comprehension Skills: • understanding meaning from context • focus attention • listening between the lines	Type: • a magazine article Comprehension Skill: • summarizing
Review of Units 6-10 page 132				

Authentic Reading	Writing	Vocabulary	Personal Expression
Type: • theater listings from *The New York Times* Comprehension Skills: • abbreviations • factual recall	Task: • a review Skill: • review of punctuation*	• movies and theaters	• favorite types of movies
Type: • newspaper excerpts from the Associated Press Comprehension Skill: • extrapolating	Task: • a news article Skill: • writing topic sentences*	• news and other media	• pros and cons of creating the news • favorite section of the newspaper
Type: • an article from *Shape Cooks* magazine Comprehension Skill: • identifying the main idea	Task: • a composition Skill: • outlining*	• restaurant language	• diet and health
Type: • real estate ads from *The New York Times* and the *Pennysaver* Comprehension Skill: • factual recall	Task: • an advertisement Skill: • prewriting technique: brainstorming*	• places of residence • building materials • parts of a house	• city living vs. country living • things that were better in the past vs. things that are better now
Type: • a newspaper article from the Associated Press Comprehension Skill: • understanding meaning from context	Task: • a composition Skill: • sequencing*	• honesty and dishonesty	• attitudes about keeping or returning found property
Type: • an article from the Internet Comprehension Skill: • factual recall	Task: • a composition Skill: • writing supporting details*	• polite and impolite	• opinions on proper etiquette
Type: • an excerpt from *Consumer Reports* Comprehension Skill: • drawing conclusions	Task: • a composition Skill: • using examples to support an argument*	• common phrasal verbs	• advantages and disadvantages of guided tours
Type: • a poem from *Chicken Soup for the Teenage Soul* Comprehension Skill: • inference and interpretation	Task: • a composition Skill: • prewriting technique: free writing*	• relationships	• qualities most important in a best friend
Type: • an article from *The New York Times* Comprehension Skill: • understanding meaning from context	Task: • a letter to the editor Skill: • writing a formal letter*	• quality of life	• opinions on stress • quality of life in hometown
Type: • jokes from *Reader's Digest* Comprehension Skill: • evaluating	Task: • a true story Skill: • writing an introduction*	• participial adjectives	• how to respond to jokes that are not funny

in Teacher's Edition

Acknowledgments

●●●●●●●●●●●●●●●●●●●●●●●●●●●●●●●●●●

The authors and series director wish to acknowledge with gratitude the following consultants, reviewers, and piloters—our partners in the development of *True Colors*.

COURSE CONSULTANTS

Berta de Llano, Puebla, Mexico • **Luis Fernando Gómez J.**, School of Education, University of Antioquia, Colombia • **Irma K. Ghosn**, Lebanese American University, Byblos, Lebanon • **Annie Hu**, Fu-Jen Catholic University, Taipei, Taiwan • **Nancy Lake**, CEL-LEP, São Paulo, Brazil • **Frank Lambert**, Pagoda Foreign Language Institute, Seoul, Korea • **Kazuhiko Yoshida**, Kobe University, Kobe City, Japan.

Reviewers and Piloters

Lucia Adrian, EF Language Schools, Miami, Florida, USA • **Ronald Aviles**, Instituto Chileno Norteamericano, Chuquicamata, Chile • **Liliana Baltra**, Instituto Chileno Norteamericano, Santiago, Chile • **Paulo Roberto Berkelmans,** CEL-LEP, São Paulo, Brazil • **Luis Beze**, Casa Thomas Jefferson, Brasília, Brazil • **Martin T. Bickerstaff**, ELS Language Centers, Oakland, California, USA • **Mary C. Black**, Institute of North American Studies, Barcelona, Spain • **James Boyd**, ECC Foreign Language Institute, Osaka, Japan • **Susan Bryan de Martínez**, Instituto Mexicano Norteamericano, Monterrey, Mexico • **Hugo A. Buitano**, Instituto Chileno Norteamericano, Arica, Chile • **Gary Butzbach**, American Language Center, Rabat, Morocco • **Herlinda Canto**, Universidad Popular Autónoma del Estado de Puebla, Mexico • **Rigoberto Castillo**, Colegio de CAFAM, Santafé de Bogotá, Colombia • **Tina M. Castillo**, Santafé de Bogotá, Colombia • **Amparo Clavijo Olarte**, Universidad Distrital, Santafé de Bogotá, Colombia • **Graciela Conocente**, Asociación Mendocina de Intercambio Cultural Argentino Norteamerica, Argentina • **Greg Conquest**, Yokohama Gaigo Business College, Japan • **Eduardo Corbo**, IETI, Salto, Uruguay • **Marilia Costa**, Instituto Brasil-Estados Unidos, Rio de Janeiro, Brazil • **Miles Craven**, Nihon University, Shizuoka, Japan • **Michael Davidson**, EF Language Schools, Miami, Florida, USA • **Celia de Juan**, UNICO, UAG, Guadalajara, Mexico • **Laura de Marín**, Centro Colombo Americano, Medellín, Colombia • **Montserrat Muntaner Djmal**, Instituto Brasil-Estados Unidos, Rio de Janeiro, Brazil • **Deborah Donnelley de García**, ITESM-Campus Querétaro, Mexico • **Rosa Erlichman**, União Cultural, São Paulo, Brazil • **Patricia Escalante Arauz**, Universidad de Costa Rica, San Pedro de Montes de Oca, Costa Rica • **Guadalupe Espinoza**, ITESM-Campus Querétaro, Mexico • **Suad Farkouh**, ESL Consultant to Philadelphia National Schools, Amman, Jordan • **Niura R.H. Ferreria**, Centro Cultural Brasil Estados Unidos, Guarapuava, Brazil • **Fernando Fleurquin**, Alianza Cultural Uruguay-EEUU, Montevideo, Uruguay • **Patricia Fleury**, Casa Thomas Jefferson, Brasília, Brazil • **Patricia Foncea**, Colegio Jesualdo, Santiago, Chile • **Areta Ulhana Galat**, Centro Cultural Brasil Estados Unidos, Curitiba, Brazil • **Christina Gitsaki**, Nagoya University of Commerce and Business Administration, Japan • **Julie Harris de Peyré**, Universidad del Valle, Guatemala • **Ruth Hassell de Hernández**, UANL, Mexico • **John Hawkes**, EF International School, Santa Barbara, California, USA • **Rose M. Hernández**, University of Puerto Rico-Bayamón, Puerto Rico • **Susan Hills**, EF International School of English, San Diego, California, USA

• **Osamu Ikeno**, Ehime University, Japan • **Jan Kelley**, EF International School, Santa Barbara, California, USA • **Mia Kim**, Kyung Hee University, Seoul, Korea • **Junko Kobayashi**, Sankei International College, Tokyo, Japan • **Gil Lancaster**, Academy Istanbul, Istanbul, Turkey • **Amy Rita Lewis**, Keio University, Tokyo, Japan • **Mónica Lobo**, Santiago, Chile • **Luz Adriana Lopera**, Centro Colombo Americano, Medellín, Colombia • **Eva Irene Loya**, ITESM-Campus Querétaro, Mexico • **Mary Maloy Lara**, Instituto John F. Kennedy, Tehuacán, Mexico • **Meire de Jesus Marion**, Associação Alumni, São Paulo, Brazil • **Juliet Marlier**, Universidad de las Américas, Puebla, Mexico • **Yolanda Martínez**, Instituto D'Amicis, Puebla, Mexico • **Neil McClelland**, Shimonoseki City University, Japan • **Regina Celia Pereira Mendes**, Instituto Brasil-Estados Unidos, Rio de Janeiro, Brazil • **Jim Miller**, Yokohama Gaigo Business College, Japan • **Milton Miltiadous**, YMCA College of English, Tokyo, Japan • **Fiona Montarry**, The American Language Center, Casablanca, Morocco • **Luiz Claudio Monteiro**, Casa Thomas Jefferson, Brasília, Brazil • **Angelita Oliveira Moreno**, ICBEU, Belo Horizonte, Brazil • **Ahmed Mohammad Motala**, King Fahd University of Petroleum & Minerals, Dhahran, Saudi Arabia • **William Richard Munzer**, Universidad IDEAS de Bogotá, Colombia • **Akiko Nakazawa**, Yokohama Gaigo Business College, Japan • **Adrian Nunn**, EF International School of English, Los Angeles, California, USA • **Margarita Ordaz Mejía**, Universidad Americana de Acapulco, Mexico • **Sherry Ou**, Fu-Jen Catholic Univ, Taipei, Taiwan • **Thelma Jonas Péres**, Casa Thomas Jefferson, Brasília, Brazil • **Renata Philippov**, Associação Alumni, São Paulo, Brazil • **Ciarán Quinn**, Otemae College, Osaka, Japan • **Ted Quock**, Keisen University, Tokyo, Japan • **Ron Ragsdale**, Bilgi University, Istanbul, Turkey • **Luís Ramírez F.**, Instituto Norteamericano de Cultura, Concepción, Chile • **Martha Restrepo Rodríguez**, Politécnico Grancolombiano, Santafé de Bogotá, Colombia • **Irene Reyes Giordanelli**, Centro Cultural Colombo Americano, Santiago de Cali, Colombia • **Dolores Rodríguez**, CELE (Centro de Lenguas), Universidad Autónoma de Puebla, Mexico • **Idia Rodríguez**, University of Puerto Rico-Arecibo, Puerto Rico • **Eddy Rojas & teachers**, Centro de Idiomas de la P. Universidad Católica, Peru • **Ricardo Romero**, Centro Cultural Colombo Americano, Santafé de Bogotá, Colombia • **Blanca Lilia Rosales Bremont**, Universidad Americana de Acapulco, Mexico • **Marie Adele Ryan**, Associação Alumni, São Paulo, Brazil • **Nadia Sarkis**, União Cultural, São Paulo, Brazil • **Andrea Seidel**, Universidad Americana de Acapulco, Mexico • **Hada Shammar**, American Language Center, Amman, Jordan • **Lai Yin Shem**, Centro Colombo Americano, Medellín, Colombia • **Maria Cristina Siqueira**, CEL-LEP, São Paulo, Brazil • **María Inés Sandoval Astudillo**, Instituto Chileno Norteamericano, Chillán, Chile • **Lilian Munhoz Soares**, Centro Cultural Brasil Estados Unidos, Santos, Brazil • **Mário César de Sousa**, Instituto Brasil-Estados Unidos, Fortaleza, Brazil • **Tatiana Suárez**, Politécnico Grancolombiano, Santafé de Bogotá, Colombia • **Richard Paul Taylor**, Nagoya University of Commerce and Business Administration, Japan • **David Thompson**, Instituto Mexicano Norteamericano de Relaciones Culturales, Guadalajara, Mexico • **Mr. Uzawa**, Sankei International College, Tokyo, Japan • **Nilda Valdez**, Centro Cultural Salvadoreño, El Salvador • **Euclides Valencia Cepeda**, Universidad Distrital, Santafé de Bogotá, Colombia • **Ana Verde**, American Language Institute, Montevideo, Uruguay • **Andrea Zaidenberg**, Step English Language Center, Argentina

Preface

•••

True Colors is a complete and articulated six-level adult or young adult course in English as a foreign language. Each book is intended to be completed in a period of 60 to 90 class hours. There are two reasons why this course is entitled *True Colors*. It presents the true voice of the native speaker of American English, and it systematically teaches students to communicate *in their own words*—to **let their true colors shine through.**

Focus and Approach

True Colors is a highly communicative international course enhanced by strong four-skills support, including an enriched and skills-based listening strand and an abundance of games, info-gaps, and other interactive activities. Short, integrated social language and grammar lessons within each unit ensure concentrated oral practice and production. *True Colors* takes into account different learning and teaching styles. It incorporates task-based strategies and is centered on the well-known fact that practice in each skill area enhances mastery of the others.

A major innovation of the *True Colors* series is to systematically build students' ability to present their own ideas, opinions, and feelings—both accurately and con-fidently. For this reason, every activity leads students to gain ownership of the language, progressively moving them *away* from models to express thoughts in their own words and to improvise based on what they know.

True Colors carefully distinguishes between receptive and productive language. It consistently presents language in the receptive mode before—and at a slightly higher difficulty level than—the productive mode. Research has shown that students are more successful when they become familiar with new language before having to produce it. Therefore, *True Colors* presents EFL students with an abundance of both receptive and productive models, combining exposure and practice for increased understanding and attainable mastery.

True Colors is specifically designed for use by students who rarely encounter English outside of class. The course is built around a wealth of speaking and reading models of the true voice of the American speaker and includes numerous authentic readings from English-language newspapers, magazines, books, and Internet sources. This refreshing change from "textbook English" is essential for students who have limited access to real native speech and writing.

Because international students do not have the opportunity to speak to native speakers on a regular basis, *True Colors* does not present activities such as interviewing native speakers or watching TV in English. Instead, the course serves as a replacement for immersion in an English-speaking environment, making the classroom itself a microcosm of the English-speaking world. The goal and promise of *True Colors* is to prepare students to move out of this textbook and to understand, speak, read, and write English in the real world.

Student Population

Book 1 of *True Colors* is written for adult and young adult false beginners. Book 2 is written at a high-beginning to low-intermediate level. Book 3 is at an intermediate level, Book 4 is at a high-intermediate level, and Book 5 concludes at an advanced level. The Basic text is an alternative entry point for true beginners or very weak false beginners.

Course Length

The *True Colors* student's books are designed to cover from 60 to 90 class hours of instruction. Although each student's book is a complete course in itself, giving presentation, practice, and production of all four skills, a full complement of supplementary components is available to further expand the material.

Components of the Course

Student's Book   The student's book is made up of ten units and two review units, one coming after Unit 5 and another coming after Unit 10.

Teacher's Edition   The teacher's edition is interleaved with the full-color student's book pages. It contains an introduction to the format and approach of *True Colors*; page-by-page teaching suggestions written especially for the teacher who teaches outside an English-speaking country; tapescripts for the audiocassettes or audio CDs; and a complete answer key to the exercises in the student's book, workbook, and achievement tests.

Teacher's Bonus Pack   The Teacher's Bonus Pack is a unique set of reproducible hands-on learning-support activities that includes duplicating masters that contain photo stories with empty speech balloons for oral and written improvisation; full-page art illustrations that recombine and recycle vocabulary, grammar, and social language from many units; learner-created grammar notes; and interactive conversation cards for social language reinforcement. The Teacher's Bonus Pack contains an array of opportunities to expand the student's book and tailor it to each classroom's particular needs.

Workbook   The workbook contains numerous additional opportunities for written reinforcement of the language taught in the student's book. The exercises in the workbook are suitable for homework or for classwork.

Audiocassettes or Audio CDs   The audiocassettes or audio CDs contain all the listening and reading texts, the conversations, the vocabulary presentations, the Listening with a Purpose texts, the Authentic Readings, and the pronunciation presentations and practices from the student's book. The cassettes and CDs provide space for student practice and self-correction.

Videocassette   The videocassette, *True Voices*, contains a unique combination of controlled dramatic episodes that support the social language and grammar in the *True Colors* student's book; excerpts from real television broadcasts; and authentic, unrehearsed discussions by ordinary people on a variety of subjects introduced in the student's book unit.

Video Workbook   A video workbook enhances comprehension and provides active language practice and reinforcement of all social language and grammar from the video.

Achievement Tests   Achievement tests offer opportunities for evaluation of student progress on a unit-by-unit basis and provide a midterm and a final test as well. In addition, a placement test is available to aid in placing groups or individuals in one of the six levels of *True Colors*: Basic, Book 1, Book 2, Book 3, Book 4, or Book 5.

Student's Book Unit Contents

Photo Story An illustrated conversation or story provokes interest, provides enjoyment, and demonstrates the use of target language in authentic, natural speech. This rich model of real speech can be presented as a reading or a listening. It is purposely designed to be a slight step ahead of students' productive ability because students can understand more than they can produce, and the EFL student needs abundant authentic models of native speech.

Comprehension Activities based on the photo story focus on the key comprehension skills of factual recall, confirmation of content, identifying main ideas, inference and interpretation, and understanding meaning from context. These activities can serve as listening comprehension or reading comprehension exercises. Additionally, students have an opportunity to express personal opinions about an aspect of the photo story or to retell the photo story to a partner, in their own words.

Grammar and Meaning A reading or listening text provides a richly contextualized presentation of the unit's grammar while introducing the theme of the unit.

Comprehension An exercise ensures comprehension of the reading or listening focus and prepares the way for the grammar presentation to follow.

Grammar presentation A concise but clearly explained presentation of the unit's target grammar provides rules for meaning and use as well as representative examples that help all types of students learn the grammar. The grammar presentations anticipate the social language and support the unit's thematic focus. Grammar therefore is

never taught in isolation, but rather forms a support for the social language and thematic focus of the unit, giving the grammar both meaning and purpose. To this end, grammar exercises are set in a context that supports the communicative focus of the unit.

Social Language Lessons Short, numbered lessons form the social language core of each unit of *True Colors*. Social language and grammar are woven through each of these "mini-lessons" through the following combination of presentations and opportunities for practice:

Conversation A short dialogue at the students' productive level presents and models important social language.

 A major goal of *True Colors* is to teach students to improvise based on the language they already know. Improvisation is the "fifth skill"—the one students need to master in order to move out of the pages of a textbook and into the real world. Improvise activities expand the Conversation, allowing for personalization and the incorporation of new contexts and situations.

Pronunciation Five of the ten units include a pronunciation section that isolates an important feature of the pronunciation or intonation of spoken American English. The emphasis is on practice of these features, and each is supported by recorded examples on the audiocassettes or audio CDs.

Game or Inter-Action Each unit contains at least one interactive language activity that activates grammar, social language, vocabulary, or pronunciation.

Listening with a Purpose In addition to the other recorded texts in the unit, one or two additional listening texts provide another receptive model a step above students' productive ability. A three-step comprehension syllabus centers on three essential listening skills—determining context, focusing attention, and listening between the lines. Through a unique and rigorous approach to listening comprehension that is similar to the reading comprehension skills of skimming, scanning, and inferring, students build their ability to understand at a level above what is normally expected of intermediate-level students.

Authentic Reading Each unit provides practice in reading authentic texts from a variety of sources: newspapers, books, magazines, brochures, advertisements, and the Internet. Selections are chosen to expand the thematic focus of the unit, to provide material to support and motivate discussion and writing, and to prepare students to cope with authentic materials. Each authentic reading is followed by further comprehension practice in reading comprehension sub-skills.

 This unique and exciting culminating activity systematically builds students' ability to express their own opinions, ideas, and feelings on a variety of topics. Carefully designed questions provoke interest without soliciting production above students' level. Each Heart to Heart activity comes at a place where students have had enough preparation for success.

Vocabulary Vocabulary sections present thematically related vocabulary to enhance students' discussions, interactions, and writings. The words are presented in a variety of ways: through pictures, with definitions, and through contextual sentences. These

presentations ensure comprehension and provide students with a model for defining and explaining new words in the future.

 **Speaking** This full-page illustration that ends each unit has been especially drawn to elicit from students all the language they have learned within the unit—the vocabulary, the social language, the grammar, and the thematic contexts. Students can ask each other questions about the actions depicted, make true and false statements about what they see, create conversations for the characters, tell stories about what is happening—all IN THEIR OWN WORDS. All students, regardless of ability, will succeed at their own levels because what the students know how to say has been included in the illustration. What they don't know how to say has been purposely left out. Furthermore, because language learning is a process of continuing activation, the In Your Own Words illustrations include opportunities to recycle and reuse vocabulary, grammar, and social language from previous units as well.

Writing Writing activities in each unit provide real and realistic writing tasks. At the same time they offer practice in paragraph and composition development that reinforces the target language while providing additional opportunities for personal expression.

Review Units These units are provided mid-book, after Unit 5, and at the end. They provide review, self-tests, extra classroom practice, and a social language self-test.

Appendices The key vocabulary, verb charts, adjective and adverb charts, and grammatical terms are organized and presented at the end of the book for easy reference and test preparation.

About the Authors and Series Director

Authors

Jay Maurer

Jay Maurer has taught English in Binational Centers, colleges, and universities in Portugal, Spain, Mexico, the Somali Republic, and the United States. In addition, he taught intensive English at Columbia University's American Language Program.

Dr. Maurer has an M.A. and an M. Ed. in Applied Linguistics as well as a Ph. D. in The Teaching of English, all from Columbia University. In addition to this new adult and young adult English course, he is the author of the Advanced Level of Longman's widely acclaimed *Focus on Grammar* series, coauthor of the three-level *Structure Practice in Context* series, and coauthor of the *True Voices* video series. Dr. Maurer teaches and writes in the Seattle, Washington, area and recently conducted a series of teaching workshops in Brazil and Japan.

Irene E. Schoenberg

Irene E. Schoenberg has taught English to international students for over twenty years at Hunter College's International Language Institute and at Columbia University's American Language Program. Additionally, she trains English instructors in EFL/ESL teaching methods at The New School for Social Research. Her M.A. is in TESOL from Columbia University. She is a popular speaker to national and international TESOL groups.

Professor Schoenberg is the author of the Basic Level of the *Focus on Grammar* series as well as the author of the two engaging, unique, and widely used conversation texts, *Talk About Trivia* and *Talk About Values*. In addition to *True Colors*, Professor Schoenberg has coauthored the *True Voices* video series.

Series Director

Joan Saslow

Joan Saslow has taught English and foreign languages to adults and young adults in both South America and the United States. She taught English at the Binational Centers of Valparaíso and Viña del Mar, Chile, and English and French at the Catholic University of Valparaíso. She taught English to Japanese university students at Marymount College and to international students in Westchester Community College's intensive program.

Ms. Saslow, whose B.A. and M.A. are from the University of Wisconsin, is author of *English in Context: Reading Comprehension for Science and Technology*, a three-level series. In addition, she has been an editor of language teaching materials, a teacher trainer, and a frequent speaker at gatherings of English teachers outside the United States for twenty-five years.

I've been looking forward to this movie.

Warm up: What kinds of things annoy you at the movies?
Read or listen. 🎧

Receptive Model

Sorry I'm late. Have you been waiting long?

Not really. Actually, I was a little late myself.

I've been looking forward to this movie. It's supposed to be hilarious. Gee, it's crowded here.

Yeah. Well, at least the movie hasn't started. I think there are two seats over there.

Excuse me. Would you mind taking off your hat?

What was that?

Could you please take off your hat?

Oh, of course. Sorry.

Can you believe that hair? Let's move.

Where?

Aren't there two seats over there in the third row?

Comprehension: Understanding Meaning from Context

Find a sentence in the photo story that is similar in meaning to each sentence below.

Example: I want to see this movie   <u>I've been looking forward to this movie.</u>

1. Could you please take off your hat? _____

2. That's a strange hairstyle. _____

3. Excuse me. _____

4. It's not that important. _____

Tell a partner what happened at the movies. Use your own words. Say as much as you can.

Example: The man and the woman met at the movies. The man was late.

GRAMMAR AND MEANING

The present perfect continuous

Receptive Model

Listening Focus • A Phone Conversation

Before You Listen: How often do you go to the movies? How often do you rent videos?
🎧 *Listen to the conversation.*

Comprehension: Factual Recall

🎧 *Listen to the conversation again. Then complete each sentence by circling the correct letter.*

1. The people talking are _____.

   a. a boss and an employee   **b.** a mother and daughter   **c.** two friends

2. The people are talking about _____.

   a. going to a movie   **b.** going out for dinner   **c.** going to a play

3. Andy and Laura are usually _____ on the weekends.

   a. unhappy   **b.** tired   **c.** busy

4. *The Touch* has been playing for _____ now.

   a. a month   **b.** a week   **c.** two weeks

The Present Perfect Continuous

Use the present perfect continuous for actions that began in the past and continue into the present. It is similar in meaning to the present perfect.

    present perfect   present perfect continuous

    I **'ve worked** here for a year.   I **'ve been working** here for a year.

The present perfect is sometimes used for actions that are completed. The present perfect continuous is not.

    I **'ve read** a book by Amy Tan. (I finished the book.)

    I **'ve been reading** a book by Amy Tan. (I'm still reading the book.)

Remember that the continuous is usually not used with non-action verbs like **be, have** (for possession), **believe, own, love, like**.

    He **has had** a car for two years. (NOT: ~~He has been having a car for two years.~~)

Compare the present perfect continuous and the simple past tense.

    She**'s been living** in Bangkok for a year. Before that, she **lived** in Cairo.

Form the present perfect continuous with **have been** or **has been** and a present participle.

            present participle

    How long **have** they **been standing** here?

GRAMMAR TASK: Find two examples of the present perfect continuous and one example of the present perfect in the photo story on pages 2-3.

4   *UNIT 1*

Grammar with a Partner

Work with a partner. Look at this outline of Jason Khan's life.

Jason Khan
- **1972:** born in Seattle
- **1983–1989:** took acting lessons
- **1987–1989:** took voice lessons
- **1990:** moved to San Francisco
- **1990–1994:** worked part-time at Campus Videos during college
- **1995:** got married and moved to New York (still lives in New York)
- **1997:** began writing movie reviews for *Film Magazine* (still writes them)

Work with a partner. Take turns asking and answering questions about Jason. Use the present perfect continuous or the simple past tense.

Example: How long / take voice lessons

    A: How long did Jason take voice lessons?
    B: He took voice lessons for two years, from 1987 to 1989.

1. How long / live in Seattle

2. How long / take acting lessons

3. How long / live in New York

4. How long / work at Campus Videos

5. How long / work for *Film Magazine*

Grammar in a Context • Verb Tense Review

Complete the conversation with the correct verb forms.

(continued on next page)

SOCIAL LANGUAGE 1

HOW TO **make polite requests/offer a favor/agree to requests**

Conversation

🎧 *Read and listen to the conversation.*

A: Would you mind keeping an eye on my things?

B: No. Not at all.

A: I'm getting something to eat. Can I get you anything?

B: Hmm . . . could you bring me a small popcorn?

A: Sure.

B: Thanks.

A: No problem.

🎧 *Listen again and practice.*

Improvise

*Work with a partner. Practice making polite requests and agreeing to them. Use **would you mind**. Use the conversation as a model.*

Some Ideas

keeping an eye on your things

giving you directions

driving you somewhere

helping you with your homework

watching your children

or your OWN idea

☑ **Now you know how to make polite requests and agree to them.**

SOCIAL LANGUAGE 2

HOW TO ask someone to repeat a request

Conversation

🎧 *Read and listen to the conversation.*

A: Could you please move over a seat?

B: What was that?

A: Would you mind moving over one seat?

B: Sorry, I can't. Someone is sitting there.

🎧 *Listen again and practice.*

Variations

What was that?
What did you say?
Sorry?
Excuse me?

Work with one or two partners.
Pretend you are at a movie, play,
concert, or sports event. It's noisy,
and you have to repeat your comments.
Decide on a situation. Create a
conversation. Use your own words.

Some Ideas

- Someone is talking.
- Someone is wearing a big hat.
- Someone has put a coat on an empty seat.
- Someone wants some candy or popcorn.

or your OWN idea

☑ **Now you know how to ask someone to repeat a request.**

SOCIAL LANGUAGE 3

How to ask for advice/make a suggestion

Conversation

🎧 *Read and listen to the conversation.*

A: Hi, Eric. What are you looking for?

B: Oh, hi. I've been trying to find a really good video. Any suggestions?

A: Have you seen *My Left Foot*? It's old, but it's supposed to be very good.

B: No, I haven't. I'll try it. Thanks.

🎧 *Listen again and practice.*

Work with a partner. You are trying to find
something (a good book, a good bakery, a
good Italian restaurant, a cheap hotel, etc.).
Ask for advice. Your partner makes
suggestions. Use the conversation as a model.

☑ **Now you know how to ask for advice and make a suggestion.**

Listening with a Purpose

Focus Attention

🎧 Look at the chart.

Movie	Type	Rating	
Close Encounters of the Third Kind	science fiction	$3\frac{1}{2}$	stars
My Fair Lady			stars
Gone With the Wind			stars
Tootsie			stars
Terminator 2			stars

4 stars (****) = excellent
3 stars (***) = good
2 stars (**) = fair
1 star (*) = terrible

🎧 Now listen to the movie reviews. As you listen, make notes on the chart.

Listening Between the Lines

🎧 Now listen between the lines to Marty Murdock's movie reviews. Pay attention to his taste in movies. Then read these two reviews from a video movie guide. Which movie do you think Marty Murdock will like better? Why?

Sound of Music, The (1965) C-174m. *** $\frac{1}{2}$: D: Robert Wise. Julie Andrews, Christopher Plummer, Eleanor Parker, Peggy Wood, Richard Haydn. Heartwarming and true story of Maria Von Trapp and the other members of the singing Von Trapp family, who must escape from the Nazis in pre-World War II Austria. Probably the biggest movie musical of all time. Good fun for the entire family, though the film's sweetness may not please everyone. Beautifully filmed in Salzburg and the Austrian Alps. Songs include "Do Re Mi," "Maria," and "Climb Ev'ry Mountain."

Star Wars (1977; re-released 1997) C-121m. *** $\frac{1}{2}$: D: George Lucas. Mark Hamill, Harrison Ford, Carrie Fisher, Peter Cushing, Alec Guinness, Kenny Baker, voice of James Earl Jones (as Darth Vader). The picture that forever changed the way science fiction movies are made. Exciting and imaginative story of Luke Skywalker, an innocent young man who becomes an interplanetary hero with the help of the mysterious "force" and his robot friends R2-D2 and C-3PO. Seven Oscars. The first of a trilogy; followed by *The Empire Strikes Back* and *Return of the Jedi*.

In Your Own Words

Listen to the movie reviews again. Take notes. Then write a review of a movie you like. Use your notes for ideas. 🎧

Authentic Reading

from *The New York Times*

Before You Read: *Do you buy theater tickets?*
Do you read advertisements for plays and movies?

Read the theater listings.

WINNER BEST MUSICAL REVIVAL
1996 TONY AWARD
Ticketmaster (212) 307-4100
Outside NY/NJ/CT: (800) 755-4000
Lou Diamond   Faith
Philips   Prince
RODGERS & HAMMERSTEIN'S

THE KING AND I
"A GREAT KING AND I!"
"MAGICAL!" —NY Magazine
Tue-Sat at 8, Mats. Wed & Sat 2, Sun 3
Groups: (212) 398-8383 or (800) 223-7565
Neil Simon Theater (+) 250 W. 52nd St.

Today at 3
Special Perf. Sunday, May 11 at 8 p.m.
For Exact Seat Locations
Tele-Charge (212) 239-6200 (24hrs/7dys)
Outside Metro NY: (800) 432-7250

CATS
Mon-Wed, Fri at 8, Sat 2 & 8, Sun 3, Wed 2
Groups: (212) 239-6262
Winter Garden Thea(+) 50th St & Bdwy

OPENS TONIGHT AT 7, Only 23 Perfs!
Blue Light Theater Co.
Clifford Odets

WAITING FOR LEFTY
Directed by JOANNE WOODWARD
Tues-Fri 8, Sat 4 & 8, Sun 7
TICKETS GOING FAST! ORDER NOW!
Call (212) 279-4200
CSC Theater 136 E. 13th St.

TOMORROW AT 8PM
GOOD SEATS AVAILABLE
Tele-charge (212) 239-6200 (24hrs/7dys)
Outside Metro NY: (800) 432-7250

MISS SAIGON
7th SENSATIONAL YEAR!
"THE SHOW IS ALREADY A LEGEND."
—Newsweek
Tickets From $15
Mon.-Sat. 8PM, Mats.: Wed. & Sat. 2PM
GROUPS 20 OR MORE:
Theater Direct: (800) 334-8457;
Group Sales Box Office:
(212) 398-8383 or (800) 223-7565
Shubert Groups: (212) 239-6262
Broadway Theater, (+) 53rd & Broadway

Source: *The New York Times*, Sunday, April 27, 1997.

Comprehension: Abbreviations

Look at the theater listings and find abbreviations (short forms) for the following words.

1. matinees (afternoon shows) ___mats___

2. performance _____

3. and _____

4. street _____

5. Tuesday _____

6. Wednesday _____

7. Friday _____

8. Saturday _____

Comprehension: Factual Recall

Read the theater listings again. With a partner, find answers to the following questions.

1. Which play has been running for seven years? _____

2. Which play hasn't opened yet? _____

3. Which play has a special show in May? _____

4. Which play is described as "magical"? _____

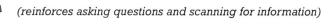

Inter-Action *(reinforces asking questions and scanning for information)*

Work with a partner. Partner A, turn to page 142. Partner B, turn to page 144.
Each of you has the back cover of a video cassette. Read about your video.
Ask about your partner's video. Tell about yours. Begin with these questions.

1. What's the name of your movie?
2. Who are the stars?
3. What's the movie about?

Heart to Heart

Ask three classmates the questions from this movie survey. Compare the students' answers. Then report your results to the class.

Movie Survey	Student 1	Student 2	Student 3
1. How often do you go to the movies?			
about once a week			
about once a month			
more than once a week			
2. What is your favorite type of movie?			
comedy			
drama			
horror			
mystery			
animated			
musical			
3. How do you choose movies?			
by reviews			
by friends' recommendations			
by the actors			
by the name of the movie			

Vocabulary

Movies and Theaters

🎧 *Look at the pictures. Say each word or phrase.*

1. the lobby
2. the refreshment stand
3. the screen
4. special effects
5. subtitles
6. the center aisle

7. the left aisle
8. the right aisle
9. the audience
10. the curtain
11. the stage
12. the cast (the actors)

13. a program
14. an usher

Seating Sections

15. the orchestra
16. the balcony

Vocabulary Practice

Read the conversation. Complete it with vocabulary words. You will not use all the words.

A: Hi, hon. I'm at the theater. Good news. There are plenty of tickets for the play tonight, and I can get us some really inexpensive seats in the _____.
  1.

B: Oh, no. Not up there! It's too far away from the _____. You can't see well enough.
  2.

A: But the seats in the _____ are really expensive.
  3.

B: I know, but I want to see the actors' faces. This play has an excellent _____.
  4.

A: OK, Let me see. . . . There are two seats in the orchestra off the center _____, row ten.
  5.

B: Great! By the way, are we going to make dinner?

A: No. I have to work late. I'll just get something at the _____. Meet me in the
  6.
_____, OK?
  7.

B: Good! See you there.

▶ **Speaking**

Warm up: Talk about the pictures with a partner. • Name as many things as you can. • Take turns asking questions about the pictures.

Then: Create conversations for the people. OR Tell a story. Say as much as you can.

Later

1 hour later

▶ **Writing:** A Review

Compare two movies. What were the names of the movies? Who starred in them? What were they about? How many stars would you give them?

13

When was Pluto discovered?

Warm up: *Do you watch television news? Or do you prefer to read a newspaper? Listen.* 🎧

5

6

Comprehension: Factual Recall

🎧 *Read the statements. Listen to the newscast again.*
Then complete each sentence by circling the correct letter.

1. The new space station was built at a cost of _____ dollars.

   a. eight billion   **b.** eighteen billion   **c.** eighty billion

2. The new planet is located more than _____ miles outside the orbit of Pluto.

   a. a million   **b.** a billion   **c.** two billion

3. _____ students were arrested for throwing eggs at the police.

   a. Twenty-two   **b.** A hundred and two   **c.** Two

4. According to a new study, one ailment caused by passive smoke is _____.

   a. cancer   **b.** AIDS   **c.** heart disease

5. Starting May 1, _____ will not be allowed on Main Street.

   a. cars   **b.** bikes   **c.** pedestrians

Listen again. Take notes. Choose one news story and tell your partner about it. Use your own words. Say as much as you can. 🎧

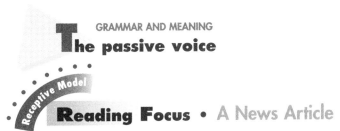

Reading Focus • A News Article

Receptive Model

Before You Read: Do you think that the news is always true? If you watch a TV newscast or read an article in a magazine, how much of it do you believe?

Read the article. (Note the examples of the passive voice in bold type.) 🎧

The News: True, False, or Somewhere in Between?

Today we live in what **is called** the Information Age. Information **is** now **considered** the most important "product." The news is everywhere — on TV and radio, in newspapers and magazines, and now even on the Internet. But can we believe it? **Can** newscasters and newswriters **be trusted?** How much of the news is true? **Is** all news just **reported,** or **is** some of it **created?** Let's examine these questions.

The first question is whether the news is true at all. You're in the supermarket checkout line, waiting to pay for your groceries. You casually pick up a tabloid and leaf through it while you're waiting. The tabloid has a headline that screams,"I **Was Captured** by Aliens!" The story **is accompanied** by a picture of a man pointing to drawings of flying saucers and strange alien creatures. "Ridiculous," you say to yourself. "Obviously false. He **was paid** to say this."

The second question is whether some of the news **is created** by reporters. If so, is that acceptable? Suppose, for example, a news organization suspects that a certain car has a defective part. Some experts have claimed that the car will catch fire in a crash. The news organization wants to prove that this will happen. Several test crashes **are filmed,** but the car never catches fire. The reporters still believe that the part is defective, though, so they meet with a mechanic and arrange to add an explosive to the car. Then a new crash **is filmed,** and the car catches fire. The news organization has "proven" that the car catches fire, but what about its methods? Some people object to this kind of activity, saying that it's dishonest. Others say that creating the news is acceptable if it's for a good reason.

There's an old saying: "Don't believe anything you hear, and only believe a quarter of what you read and half of what you see." Maybe this isn't such bad advice.

Read the article again. Then tell a partner some things that can be wrong with the news. Use your own words. Say as much as you can.

Comprehension: Inference and Interpretation

Look at the last paragraph of the article. What are some things you hear? Things you read? Things you see? Why is it safer to believe things you see than things you read?

Talk with a partner. Compare your opinions.

Is it wrong to create the news, even if it's for a good reason? What are some good reasons?

The Passive Voice

Active and passive sentences can have similar meanings, but a different focus.

> The police **arrested** the students. (active voice)

> The students **were arrested** by the police. (passive voice)

The passive voice is formed with **be** + the past participle.

> Coffee **is grown** in Brazil. (present passive)

> *Hamlet* **was written** by William Shakespeare. (past passive)

> A concert **will be performed** at Austin Hall next Friday evening. (future passive)

Use **by** when you mention the agent.

> He was hit **by** a truck.
>   ‾‾‾‾‾‾
>   agent

In newspaper headlines, the passive voice is often shortened by deleting the verb **be.**

> Movie Star Captured by Aliens

GRAMMAR TASK: Look back at the reading on page 16. Find a sentence in the passive voice that mentions the agent.

Grammar in a Context 1

Complete the conversation with the present or past passive of the indicated verbs.

Anything interesting in the paper?

Yeah. Remember Sophia Clark from my high school?

Sure—the animal rights activist.

Well, she and nineteen other people _____ last Tuesday.
1. arrest

Really? Why?

They _____ trespassing at the animal research center at the university.
2. catch

Does it say anything else about Sophia?

Uh-huh. She's become the president of Animals Feel. She _____ yesterday as saying, "Our group objects to all research using animals. The animals in research centers _____ badly. We won't stop protesting until all animal research centers _____."
3. quote
4. treat
5. close

That's nonsense. Doesn't she realize how much animal research has done for medicine? You know, heart bypass surgery _____ first on dogs.
6. do
Sophia's own dad is alive today thanks to heart bypass surgery.

I guess you're right, but I still hate it when animals _____.
7. hurt

Grammar in a Context 2

Read the headlines. Match each headline with the correct article. Then complete the articles with the passive voice of the verbs in parentheses.

Mom Saved by Three-Year-Old Daughter

Billions Spent on Space Travel

Street Fair to Be Held in Pedestrian Mall

Treasure Found in Abandoned House

1.

Street Fair to Be Held in Pedestrian Mall

Next Sunday a street fair __will be held__
                                (hold)
in the new pedestrian mall on Main Street.

Music _____ by students from
              (provide)
the university marching band.

2.

_____

Yesterday afternoon Mrs. Iris Cohn

fell in the shower and hit her head.

She _____ by her three-year-old
         (save)
daughter Gabriella, who called the

police and asked for help.

3.

_____

Every year, billions of dollars

_____ on space travel.
     (spend)
Is that right when millions

of people are hungry here

on Earth?

4.

_____

Last Sunday a locked treasure chest _____
                                          (find)
in the abandoned house at 546 Dearborn Street.

It _____ to the police station. Diamonds and
      (take)
emeralds worth more than two million dollars

_____ in the chest. The last person to be seen
  (discover)
in the house was Sam Nelson, a homeless man.

Bonus Question: Editorials are articles that express the opinion of the newspaper's editor. Which excerpt is probably the start of an editorial?

Heart to Heart

I think... *In my opinion...* *It depends.* *I'm for...*

Talk with a partner. Compare your opinions.

What section of the newspaper do you most like to read? The front page? The sports section? Editorials? Why?

I feel... *I'm against...* *What about you?*

HOW **TO** ask about rules/express certainty

Conversation

🎧 *Read and listen to the conversation.*

A: Are you allowed to park here?

B: No, you're not.

A: Are you sure?

B: I'm positive. There's a
"No Parking" sign right there.

A: Oh. I'm glad you saw it.

🎧 *Listen again and practice.*

Variations

I'm positive.
I'm sure.
I'm absolutely sure.
I'm certain.
Absolutely.

Impr...

*Work with a partner. Your partner asks
if something is allowed. You explain
why you're certain it is or isn't allowed.
Use these signs or your own ideas. Use
the conversation as a model.*

☑ **Now you know how to ask about rules and express certainty.**

HOW **TO** ask for and give an opinion

Conversation

🎧 *Read and listen to the conversation.*

A: How do you feel about video games?

B: What do you mean?

A: Do you think video games are bad for kids?

B: Not at all. I'm all for them. They're fun and they're
educational. Why? Do you think they're bad?

A: It depends. I'm against having them in schools, but
I think they're OK at home.

🎧 *Listen again and practice.*

Work with a partner. Find out how your partner feels about an issue—for example, video games in schools, animal research centers, violent movies, or money spent on space travel. Use the conversation as a model.

☑ **Now you know how to ask for and give an opinion.**

Pronunciation

Stress and Meaning

Look at the following words. Note that the stress is on the first syllable of the nouns and the second syllable of the verbs.

🎧 *Listen and repeat.*

Noun	Verb
prótest	protést
óbject	objéct
pérmit	permít
cónflict	conflíct

🎧 *Now listen to each sentence. Listen to the stress on the underlined words. Mark the stress.*

1. Students are planning a <u>protest</u> against the elimination of video games in the cafeteria.

2. Members of Animals Feel are going to <u>protest</u> the use of animals in research.

3. The <u>object</u> of the study is to find out the effects of passive smoking.

4. Some people <u>object</u> to spending large amounts of money on space exploration.

5. You'll need a <u>permit</u> to open a restaurant.

6. They won't <u>permit</u> you to drive on Main Street.

7. Last weekend there was a serious <u>conflict</u> between the students and the administration.

8. I want to see both *The Touch* and *Air Force Two*, but I can't because they're both showing at 7:00. The two movies <u>conflict</u>.

🎧 *Listen again and repeat.*

Test Your Knowledge

(reinforces passive voice)

Divide into two teams. Team A asks Team B eight questions. Then Team B asks Team A eight questions. Get one point for each question that uses the passive voice correctly. Get one point for each correct answer.

Example: the pyramids / build in

    a. Babylon
    b. Egypt
    c. Greece

A: Were the pyramids built in Babylon, Egypt, or Greece?

B: They were built in Egypt.

Be careful! Some questions need to be asked in the present. Answers are on page 142.

Team A's Questions

1. the *Mona Lisa* / paint / by
    a. Michelangelo
    b. Leonardo da Vinci
    c. Tintoretto

2. *War and Peace* / write / by
    a. Shakespeare
    b. Cervantes
    c. Tolstoy

3. the United Nations / establish / in
    a. 1945
    b. 1940
    c. 1950

4. diamonds / mine / in
    a. South Africa
    b. Egypt
    c. Japan

5. the ancient Olympics / hold / in
    a. Rome
    b. Alexandria
    c. Athens

6. Pompeii / destroy / by
    a. a volcano
    b. an earthquake
    c. a fire

7. the electric light / invent / by
    a. Bell
    b. Edison
    c. Marconi

Team B's Questions

1. the *Moonlight Sonata* / compose / by
    a. Beethoven
    b. Mozart
    c. Rachmaninoff

2. paper / invent / by
    a. the Japanese
    b. the Egyptians
    c. the Chinese

3. *Antony and Cleopatra* / write / by
    a. Cervantes
    b. Boccaccio
    c. Shakespeare

4. the Statue of Liberty / build / by
    a. the English
    b. the French
    c. the Americans

5. bananas / grow / in
    a. Iceland
    b. the Philippines
    c. Canada

6. the movie *Rashomon* / direct / by
    a. Steven Spielberg
    b. Federico Fellini
    c. Akira Kurosawa

7. the Basque language / speak / in
    a. Japan and Korea
    b. Spain and France
    c. Uruguay and Paraguay

Authentic Reading
from the Associated Press

Before You Read: *Think about a newspaper you have read lately. What articles did you like most?*

Read the excerpts. 🎧

She gives hosp 2M

ROCKFORD, Ill. — A reclusive woman has left $2.3 million to the hospital where she worked for 34 years as a part-time clerk. Helen Howell, who died Sept. 2 at 72, was a frugal woman who ate TV dinners and drove a 10-year-old car.

Source: The Associated Press

Born in the fast lane

By SCOTT SUNDE
P-I REPORTER

Talk about your freeway rush hour.

Camryn Buck—all of 6 pounds, 4 ounces—proved as impatient as any road-raged motorist as she entered the world with a healthy cry along the side of Interstate 405 in Bellevue yesterday afternoon.

Camryn's parents, Brian and Julie Buck of Renton, hoped to make it to Group Health's hospital in Redmond in time for the birth of their second child.

Source: The Associated Press

In Your Own Words Choose one of the articles. What do you think happened next? Write another paragraph for the article. Use your own words. Say as much as you can.

Listening with a Purpose

Focus Attention

Look at the chart.

Location	Weather
The Caribbean	hurricane
The New England states and southeastern Canada	
Western Europe	
Russia, Poland, and the Scandinavian countries	
The Far East	
Southern South America	

🎧 *Now listen to the weather report. Listen for the weather in each place. As you listen, make notes on the chart.*

Vocabulary

News and Other Media

Say each word or phrase. Study the definitions.

an editor: The editor of a newspaper supervises the reporters.

The **editor** didn't like the reporter's last story.

a publisher: The publisher of a newspaper is its owner.

Alex Turner owns this paper. He's the **publisher.**

an editorial: An editorial is an article that expresses the opinion of the newspaper's editor.

Ms. Jasper wrote an **editorial** on the use of animal research.

the media: Organizations that present the news (radio, TV, newspapers, and magazines) are called the media.

I think the **media** usually get their facts right.

run: A person who controls or manages a business or organization runs it.

Barbara Allen **runs** the editorial department.

cover: To cover a story is to go to an event, talk to people, take notes, and then write the story.

Our reporters **cover** all the major news stories in this town.

a protest

a reporter

an edition

Vocabulary Practice

Read this article by a person who works at a newspaper. Fill in the blanks with vocabulary words. Use each word or phrase only once.

I'm a _____ at the *Lewisberg Examiner*. I love my job.
1.

The *Examiner* comes out in the morning, and the early _____ is delivered by 6 or 7 A.M.
2.

This is a great place to work. Stanford Blake is the _____ of the *Examiner*; he pays
3.

the bills. But Nancy Grant, the _____, is the person who really _____ the place.
4. **5.**

Right now I'm helping Ms. Grant with an _____ she's writing on the new tax
6.

increases. The group "Citizens for Fair Taxation" is planning a _____ tomorrow, which
7.

I'm going to _____. I'll get some information that will help Ms. Grant form her opinion.
8.

People in the _____ are criticized a lot these days. I'm sure that there are some
9.

bad newspaper reporters. But most of us try hard to do our jobs well.

Mike Morris, reporter

▶ Speaking

Warm up: Talk about the picture with a partner. • Take turns asking questions. • Who are the people? What are they doing? What do they want?

Then: Create conversations for the people. OR Tell a story. Say as much as you can.

In Your Own Words

ACME CHEMLABS

ACME CHEMLABS

STOP ANIMAL TESTING!

ANIMALS FEEL, TOO!

BE KIND TO ANIMALS

NO PARKING ZONE

How do you feel about animal research?

CLOSE ALL ANIMAL RESEARCH CENTERS

FAIR VALLEY NEWS

FAIR VALLEY NEWS

▶ Writing: A News Article

Write a news article based on the picture on this page. Include a headline. Make your article exciting. Include as many details as you can. Note: News articles use short paragraphs.

Unit 3

This lunch might end up costing me an arm and a leg.

Receptive Model

Warm up: Do you enjoy preparing food for people?
Read or listen. 🎧

Alice, that meal you made last night was out of this world.

Thanks. . . . It <u>was</u> pretty good, wasn't it?

Uh-huh. What's up? This kitchen looks like a hurricane hit it.

I've started a catering business. If all goes well, I may be saying good-bye to the phone company forever.

Wow, that's great. By the way, how did you get into this?

Really? Well, how's the business going?

Well, everyone knew I loved cooking. Then out of the blue about two months ago I got a call to cater a party.

And since then, I've had a catering job practically every weekend.

So far so good. I got a call this morning from someone asking me to cater a dinner for twenty.

That's so neat. Want some help?

Comprehension: Inference and Interpretation

Read the statements. Put a check next to the three sentences that are probably true.

1. ☑ Alice works for the telephone company.

2. ☑ A caterer cooks for other people.

3. ☒ Alice doesn't want to quit her job.

4. ☑ Portobellos are a kind of mushroom.

5. ☐ It's easy to make money in a catering business.

Tell a partner about Alice and her business.
Use your own words. Say as much as you can.

Example: Alice has always loved cooking. Now she's started . . .

May and might and tag questions

Listening Focus • A Radio Program

Before You Listen: What are some of your favorite foods? Are they good for you?

🎧 Listen to the radio program.

Comprehension: Factual Recall

🎧 Listen to the radio program again. Then complete each statement by circling the correct letter.

1. The program is about _____.

   a. food and health   **b.** good restaurants and   **c.** fruits and vegetables
                               bad restaurants

2. The speaker discusses _____.

   a. candy and desserts   **b.** meat and vegetables   **c.** bread and pasta

3. She talks about _____.

   a. drinks only   **b.** foods only   **c.** foods and drinks

4. According to Penelope Goodenough, uncooked or partially cooked _____ might contain harmful bacteria.

   a. vegetables   **b.** meat   **c.** pasta

5. Penelope Goodenough says that _____ meat may be safer to eat.

   a. uncooked   **b.** partially cooked   **c.** thoroughly cooked

6. Drinking orange juice may be almost as good as eating _____.

   a. an orange   **b.** a grape   **c.** an apple

7. Red wine might be _____ for the heart.

   a. bad   **b.** good   **c.** necessary

8. According to Penelope Goodenough, drinking grape juice might prevent _____.

   a. cancer   **b.** headaches   **c.** heart attacks

May **and** Might

Look at this diagram.

0% ←——————————————————————————————→ 100%

won't   may OR might   will probably   will

Use **may** or **might** to show a possibility in the present or future.

> She **may** be at home.

> I **might** start a catering business.

The negative of **may** is **may not.** The negative of **might** is **might not.**

> They **may not** come to dinner. We **might not** eat out tonight.

TIP: **May** and **might** don't have -**s** in the third person singular.

Don't use **to** immediately after **may** and **might.** Use the base form.

GRAMMAR TASK: Find two statements with **may** or **might** in the photo story on pages 26–27. In your own words, say each one in another way.

Grammar in a Context

A. Complete the conversation with **might** or **might not** and the verb **call.**

Hi, honey. Wow, what a day. How about going out to eat tonight?

OK. Good idea. Oh, but wait. . . . Danny said he _____ this evening.
1.

Mark, you know how Danny is. He _____ in a few minutes, or he _____ at midnight.
2.
3.
Or he _____ at all.
4.

Yeah, you're right. Let's go.

B. Complete the conversation with **may** or **may not** and the indicated verbs.

Hello?

Hi, Karen. It's me. I just finished work. You and the kids had better leave for the picnic now. I _____ home in time for all of us to go together. I'll just go from work.
1. get

Well, OK, but do you know how to get there?

Well, Frank said he was going to the picnic, too. He _____ still _____
2. be
here. If he is, I'll follow him.

Tag Questions

We often use tag questions after statements when we think we know the answer to a question. They mean, "Isn't that true?" or "Right?" Tag questions are the same tense as the statement.

statement   tag question
You live in Winnipeg, ***don't you?*** (simple present)

statement   tag question
You haven't met my daughter, ***have you?*** (present perfect)

statement   tag question
You're coming to dinner tonight, ***aren't you?*** (present continuous)

statement   tag question
You didn't go there, ***did you?*** (simple past)

If the statement is affirmative, the tag is negative.

If the statement is negative, the tag is affirmative.

TIP: Answer tag questions the same way you answer other ***yes-no*** questions.

         You live in Bellevue, don't you?   Yes, I do.

GRAMMAR TASK: Find a tag question in the photo story on pages 26–27. Then find the answer.

Grammar in a Context

Complete each conversation with tag questions.

Let's see. You ordered the stuffed octopus, __didn't you__, ma'am?
1.

No, I didn't. I ordered the spicy snails.

Let's go somewhere different tonight.

OK. You haven't been to the Pink Lotus, __have you__?
2.
Their food is out of this world.

Troy won't eat vegetables. I don't know what to do.

Well, he likes fruit, __doesn't he__? Try that.
3.
It'll give him just as many vitamins.

You guys aren't leaving already, __are you__?
4.
We're just getting started.

Yeah, unfortunately. Dave's got an early flight to Phoenix. We had a great time, though.

Look at your picture for one minute. Then close your book and make statements with tag questions about your picture. Your partner looks at your picture and answers. Then reverse roles.

Partner A's Picture

Partner B's Picture

Example: The man is reading a newspaper, isn't he?

SOCIAL LANGUAGE 1

HOW TO ask and tell about an occupation

Conversation

🎧 *Read and listen to the conversation.*

A: What do you do?

B: I have a catering business.

A: How did you first get into that?

B: Well, cooking was my hobby.
And one thing led to another. What about you?

A: I'm a full-time mom.

B: That's great. How many kids do you have?

A: Two.

🎧 *Listen again and practice.*

Work with a partner. Find out how your partner first got interested in his or her occupation or hobby. Use the conversation as a model.

Some Ideas

a graphic designer

a full-time mom or dad

a financial adviser

a restaurant manager

a magician

or your OWN idea

☑ **Now you know how to ask and tell about an occupation or hobby.**

HOW TO **ask for and give an opinion/confirm location**

Conversation

🎧 *Read and listen to the conversation.*

A: How's that new Indian restaurant?

B: So-so. The food's OK, but the service is lousy. If you like Indian food, why don't you try Delhi Gardens? It's a lot better.

A: That's next to the movie theater, isn't it?

B: Yes. You can't miss it.

🎧 *Listen again and practice.*

Improvise

Talk with a partner. Ask about a new restaurant in town. Use the conversation as a model.

Some Ideas

the atmosphere · the bathrooms · the service

the food · the location · or your OWN idea

☑ **Now you know another way to ask for and give an opinion. You also know how to confirm location.**

Receptive Model

Authentic Reading

from *Shape Cooks* magazine

Before You Read: What foods or drinks are good for your health? Describe their benefits.

Read the article.

A Good Cup of Tea

Coffee drinkers take note. Tea—that drink with jam and bread—might reduce one's risk of stroke by as much as 73 percent. The *Archives of Internal Medicine* recently reported on a study in the Netherlands of 550 men, which showed that those who drank five cups of black tea a day had the lowest risk of stroke. Scientists believe flavonoids, nonnutritive compounds found abundantly in tea (and in fruits and vegetables), act as antioxidants against arterial-blocking cholesterol.

Popular belief in Asia has long asserted the benefits of tea in preventing every malady from tooth decay to cancer, but until now research has found evidence that only green tea might help prevent cancer—but so far only in lab mice.

—*Gregory Orr*

Reprinted with permission from *Shape Cooks* magazine, Summer 1997.

Comprehension: Identifying the Main Idea

*All of the following statements are true. One of them is the main idea of the reading and the others are details. Mark the main idea **M**. Mark the details **D**.*

1. _____ Flavonoids are believed to be antioxidants.

2. _____ Cancer and tooth decay are maladies.

3. _____ Tea may be good for your health.

4. _____ Some scientists are studying flavonoids.

5. _____ Green tea might help prevent cancer.

Talk with a partner about coffee, tea, or another drink. How do you prepare it? Does it have any health benefits? Use the Authentic Reading as a model.

Listening with a Purpose

Listening Between the Lines

🎧 *Listen to the discussion between four people in a restaurant.*

🎧 *Now listen between the lines. Listen for each speaker's opinion. Then answer the questions.*

1. What does one man mean when he says, "There's always a new health fad"?

_____

2. What does the woman mean when she says, "I'll bet it's loaded with fat—about three million grams"?

_____

3. What does the other woman mean when she says, "I don't know why you guys don't both look like balloons"?

_____

Discuss the answers with your class.

Talk with a partner. Compare your opinions.

Do some people worry too much about food and health? Give your partner some examples from your experience.

Vocabulary

Restaurant Language

🎧 *Say each word or phrase. Study the definitions.*

a meal: A meal is food prepared for breakfast, lunch, or dinner.
   Most people eat three **meals** a day.

a course: A course is a part of a meal.
   This dinner has three **courses**: soup, a main dish, and dessert.

an appetizer: An appetizer is a small course that begins some meals.
   My favorite **appetizer** is soup.

an entrée: "Entrée" is another name for "main dish" or "main course."
   Chicken is a common **entrée.**

a reservation: A reservation is a promise from a restaurant to save you a table at a specific time.
   We called for a **reservation,** but the restaurant was full.

a tip: A tip is money for the waiter or waitress to show satisfaction with his or her service.
   We left the waiter a big **tip** because he did his job very well.

fast food: Fast food is food that is prepared and served quickly and informally, usually in a self-service restaurant (sometimes called a fast-food restaurant).
   I didn't have much time for lunch, so I just went out for **fast food.**

junk food: Junk food is food that may taste good but isn't very good for your health.
   If I eat too much **junk food,** I don't feel well.

gain weight: Someone who has gained weight weighs more now than in the past.
   I'm not going to eat dessert because I don't want to **gain weight.**

lose weight: Someone who has lost weight weighs less now than in the past.
   If you eat less food than your body needs, you will **lose weight.**

nutritious: Nutritious food is food that is good for your health.
   Spinach is a **nutritious** vegetable.

Vocabulary Practice

Read the letter. Fill in the blanks with vocabulary words. Use the correct word form.

Dear Mom,

I had the most wonderful time tonight. Ben called yesterday and asked if he

could take me to dinner and a play to celebrate our engagement. Of course I

said yes. I thought we'd just get some _____ before we
                                          1.

went to the theater. Boy, was I surprised! He took me to the most expensive

restaurant in town. We had a _____ for the nicest table
                                      2.

in the place, and the dinner was five separate

_____ .
          3.

Mom, I think it was the best food I've ever eaten.

For an _____ , we had a bowl
                  4.

of spicy vegetable soup. The _____
                                        5.

was poached salmon with hollandaise sauce—absolutely

delicious. I definitely _____
                                   6.

weight tonight! It's all right, though. It was healthy,

_____ food. They don't serve
          7.

_____ at this restaurant.
          8.

Our waiter was very helpful and friendly, so Ben

left him fifteen dollars for a _____ .
                                          9.

This was a meal I'll never forget.

I'll write again soon.

Love, Magda

▶ **Speaking**

Warm up: Talk about the picture with a partner. • Where are the people? • What are they doing? • What are they eating? • What are the occupations of the two men on the right? • Are reservations necessary at this restaurant?

Then: Study the picture for a minute. Close your eyes. Ask your partner five tag questions about the picture. Your partner does the same. • Create conversations for the people. OR Tell a story. Say as much as you can.

In Your Own Words

How's this restaurant?

▶ **Writing:** A Composition

Write about your favorite restaurant or your favorite home-cooked meal. Describe the food. If you are writing about a restaurant, tell why the restaurant is special.

Unit 4

I don't make as much money as I used to.

Warm up: Do you prefer living in the city or living in the country?
Listen. 🎧

Comprehension: Understanding Meaning from Context

Look at the underlined phrases. Then listen to the conversation again. Match each underlined phrase with its meaning.

1. Now I <u>telecommute</u>.

2. But I was just totally <u>stressed out</u> in town.

3. Isn't it kind of tough financially, though, trying to <u>make it on your own</u>?

4. It sounds like <u>the middle of nowhere</u>.

5. Hey, you <u>ought to</u> come out some time and visit.

a. should

b. work without regular pay from a company

c. work from home on a computer

d. a place where not many people live

e. very nervous and upset

 **Tell a partner about the recent changes in Jerry's life. Use your own words. Say as much as you can.**

Reading Focus • A Newspaper Article

Before You Read: *Think of some advantages and disadvantages of cities and small towns.*

Read the newspaper article. (Note the examples of **used to** *and comparisons with* **as** *in bold type.)* 🎧

The St. Louis Intelligencer

Hustle and Bustle or the Middle of Nowhere?

In our continuing series about modern lifestyles, we look today at town and country: the urban lifestyle versus the rural one. We interviewed two individuals, one who went from the country to the city and one who did the reverse. Part 5 in the series.

Janet Lincoln is an accountant who moved to St. Louis five years ago and loves living here. Here's what Janet told us:

"Five years ago I **used to** live in a small town called Lemon Falls out in the western part of the state. I grew up and went to high school there. After I graduated I worked for a year in a supermarket, which was one of three stores in the town. Lemon Falls had a population of about 800 people, and I knew every single one of them. They all knew everything about me, too. There was no privacy. You couldn't do anything or go anywhere without everyone in town knowing about it. The first chance I got I moved to St. Louis, and I love

it. I don't know **as many people** now **as** I **used to,** but that's OK. I have a few good friends, and I see them when I want to. I kind of like being anonymous. There are lots of great cultural activities in the city, like the theater and the symphony. I'd never go back to Lemon Falls."

Troy Henson had the opposite experience. A lifelong city resident, he and his wife, Darla, and their two children moved from St. Louis to Bloomfield three years ago. Here's what Troy told us:

"The best thing we ever did was get out of St. Louis. Don't get me wrong; St. Louis is **as good a place as** any other city, I suppose—if you like cities, that is. We don't. Both Darla and I grew up in St. Louis and went to college there. We met at college and got married. Then the kids came along and life got pretty challenging. Both Darla and I were working, so we had to put the kids in day care. We lived in an apartment building, and

we didn't know any of our neighbors. We both had good jobs, but it always seemed like there was never enough money. That all changed when we moved to Bloomfield. Darla works part-time and stays home with the kids the rest of the time. I don't make **as much money as** I **used to,** but then we don't have **as many expenses as** we did. We know our neighbors. We're part of a community. The schools here are just **as good as** the schools in St. Louis— maybe better. Life is good. We'd never leave Bloomfield."

It occurs to us at *The Intelligencer* that the basic question here is not really city living versus country living; it's whether you're a private person or a public person. Maybe some people just don't need **as much privacy as** others do. It's food for thought, anyway.

Tomorrow: Part 6 in the series: "Home Schooling: Is It for You?"

In Your Own Words

What does Janet Lincoln like about life in the city? What does Troy Henson dislike about life in the city? Tell a partner. Use your own words. Say as much as you can.

Comprehension: Understanding Grammar from Context

Circle the choice closer in meaning to each sentence from the reading.

1. I don't know as many people now as I used to.

    a. I knew more people before.   **b.** I know more people now.

2. I don't make as much money as I used to.

    a. I make more money now.   **b.** I made more money before.

3. We don't have as many expenses as we did.

    a. Life was more expensive in the past.   **b.** Life was less expensive in the past.

Comparisons with As

adjectives and adverbs

Use **as** + adjective or adverb + **as** to talk about things that are equal in some way.

> The white house is **as old as** the red one. They're both twelve years old.

Use **not as** + adjective or adverb + **as** to talk about things that are different in some way.

> The white house is **not as old as** the yellow one. The yellow house is twenty years old. The white house is twelve years old.

> He does**n't** drive **as slowly as** I do.

▼ **T I P :** *Just* is often used in comparisons of equality.

> The schools here are **just as good as** the schools in town.

count nouns

Use **as many** + count noun + **as** to talk about things that are equal in some way.

> There are **as many problems** in the country **as** there are in the city.

Use **not as many** + count noun + **as** to talk about things that are different in some way.

> The green house does**n't** have **as many rooms as** the white one.

non-count nouns

Use **as much** + non-count noun + **as** to talk about things that are equal in some way.

> The drive took **as much time as** we expected.

Use **not as much** + non-count noun + **as** to talk about things that are different in some way.

> The brick house does**n't** need **as much work as** the white one.

GRAMMAR TASK: Look back at the example sentences in this box. Say three sentences again. Use your own adjective or adverb, count noun, and non-count noun.

Grammar in a Context

*Complete the conversation with **as, as many,** or **as much.***

Hey, nice car.

Thanks. I like it too. It's not _____as_____ big
1.
as my old car.

And I'll bet it doesn't need _as much_ gas, either.
2.

By the way, where do you keep it?

In a garage. Since they opened those new stores, there aren't _as many_
3.
parking spaces as there used to be.

I heard you went out to Jerry Lima's.

Yeah, I was there last Sunday. You know, Monroe isn't nearly _____as_____ far as I thought. It
4.
only took me an hour and a half to get there.

What's his house like? Is it _____as_____ nice as he says?
5.

Nicer . . . that is, if you like the country.

InterAction *(reinforces comparisons with **as**)*

*Work with a partner. Partner A is in favor of country living. Partner B is in favor of city living. Discuss the advantages and disadvantages of each. Use comparisons with **as**. Here are some words you may want to use.*

Adjectives	Count Nouns	Non-count Nouns	Verbs and Adverbs

Adjectives	Count Nouns	Non-count Nouns	Verbs and Adverbs
crowded	factories	crime	drive far
clean	cultural activities	pollution	shop easily
convenient	hospitals	noise	sleep late
exciting	jobs	smog	wake up early
quiet	people	stress	work hard
safe	schools	traffic	

Example: **A:** The city isn't as quiet as the country. That's a disadvantage of living in the city.

B: That's true, but the country can be boring. It's never as exciting as the city.

Used To

Use **used to** + base form to tell about repeated actions in the past that no longer happen or to tell about facts or conditions in the past that are no longer true.

> He **used to wear** a suit and tie to work.

> We **used to have** a home in the country. (We don't have it anymore.)

Do not use **used to** + base form for a specific time in the past.

> He bought a house three years ago. (NOT: ~~He used to buy a house three years ago.~~)

Be careful! Note the spelling of **use** in questions: Didn't you use (not ~~used~~) to live in the city?

GRAMMAR TASK: Look back at the reading on page 40. Find two sentences with **used to**. Say them in another way. Start with **In the past . . .**

Grammar in a Context

*Complete the conversation. Use **used to** + the base form of the verb wherever possible. Use the simple past tense in other cases.*

Hi, Sarah. This is Rich. How about dinner tonight?

I'd love to, but I've got a pile of work to do. My boss ___gave___ me a new
1. give
assignment. Tomorrow?

I can't tomorrow. I'm going to be away on business.

You know, before we ___got___ these fabulous
2. get
jobs, we had a much better life. We ___used to have___
3. have
dinner out once or twice a week. We ___used to go___
4. go
to concerts at least once a month, and we
___we used to see___ friends all the time.
5. see

That's true, but in those days we were always broke.

Talk with a partner about the way things used to be for you.
What was better then? What's better now?

Example: When I was younger, I used to stay out until four in the morning, and I used to sleep until noon. That was better than today—now I have to get up early.

SOCIAL LANGUAGE 1
HOW TO **confirm information/emphasize an opinion**

Conversation

🎧 *Read and listen to the conversation.*

A: Didn't you use to work at the bank?
B: Yes, but I really didn't like it.
Now I work at home.
A: Do you like it better?
B: Absolutely. Take it from me—
it's a lot better to work at
home than in an office.

🎧 *Listen again and practice.*

Variations

Take it from me—
Believe me—
Take my word for it—

Impr...

*Improvise conversations with classmates.
Ask about things you think they used to do.
Use the conversation as a model.*

☑ **Now you know how to confirm information and emphasize an opinion.**

SOCIAL LANGUAGE 2
HOW TO **express surprise at a change**

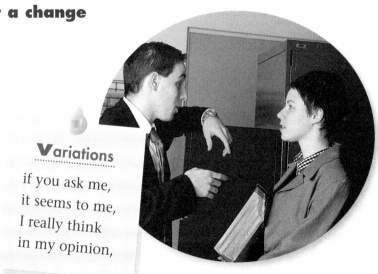

Conversation

🎧 *Read and listen to the conversation.*

A: I heard Bill's quitting.
B: Bill? I can't believe it. Why in the
world would he do that?
A: Well, he said he needed a change.
B: I wish him luck, but if you ask me,
he's making a big mistake.

🎧 *Listen again and practice.*

Variations

if you ask me,
it seems to me,
I really think
in my opinion,

44   UNIT 4

Improvise

Have a conversation with a partner. You (or someone you know) has made a big change. Your partner thinks the change was a mistake. Use the conversation as a model.

Some Ideas

The person is:
- moving
- getting married
- getting divorced
- changing jobs

or your OWN idea

☑ **Now you know how to express surprise at a change.**

Pronunciation

Didn't you, Wouldn't you, Don't you, Can't you

*In informal conversation, it is natural for people to pronounce **t** + **y** as a /tʃ/ sound.*

🎧 *Listen to the conversations.*

1. A: Didn't you use to work at The Wrap?
B: Yes, I did.

2. A: Don't you think it's important to plan ahead?
B: No, I don't.

3. A: Wouldn't you like to live on a ship?
B: No way. I hate the sea.

4. A: Can't you do that tomorrow?
B: Well, I guess so.

🎧 *Listen again and repeat.*

Now work with a partner. Take turns. Ask your partner the questions. Practice the /tʃ/ sound.

Bonus Ask your own question. Begin with *Didn't you, Wouldn't you, Don't you,* or *Can't you.*

Receptive Model

Authentic Reading

from *The New York Times* and the *Pennysaver*

Before You Read: Describe your house or apartment.

Read the ads. 🎧

House for Sale
EAST FISHKILL 1 acre $165,000 3 BR, 2.5 baths, pvt bath in MBR Country Kitchen w/brick fplc, enclosed porch, cedar family rm, 2 car gar, near all parkways and trains. By appointment.

Source: *Pennysaver/Kingsbridge,* June 21, 1997.

Apartment for Sale
200s West
EXCLUSIVE LISTING
Spectacular river view, high floor, 3BR 2 baths, state of the art kitchen, extra lge terrace, abundant closets. Luxury bldg, pool, avail prkg.....$325,000.
SHELLEY SCHERMAN
Realtor   718-549-0100

Source: *The New York Times,* October 19, 1997.

Comprehension: Factual Recall

A. *Look back at the Authentic Reading on page 45. Answer these questions about the house.*

1. How many bedrooms are there in the house? _____

2. Where is the fireplace? _____

3. How many cars fit in the garage? _____

4. How much land comes with the house? _____

B. *Answer these questions about the apartment.*

1. What can you see from the apartment? _____

2. Why is it so expensive? List two things. _____

3. How do you know that the kitchen is modern? _____

4. How many bathrooms are there in this apartment? _____

C. *Now make comparisons with **as**.*

Example: rooms _____*The apartment doesn't have as many rooms as the house.*_____

1. expensive _____

2. bathrooms _____

3. bedrooms _____

Listening with a **Purpose**

Receptive Model

Focus Attention 1

Look at the chart.

House 1: Maple Street		House 2: 28th Avenue	
Rent per month	1800	Rent per month	$ 900
Number of bedrooms	2	Number of bedrooms	2
Number of bathrooms	2	Number of bathrooms	1
Access to public transportation		Access to public transportation	No
Pets allowed?		Pets allowed?	allowed

🎧 *Listen to the conversation with a real-estate agent. Listen for information about each house. Make notes on the chart.*

Focus Attention 2

Now listen to the conversation again. Then complete each statement by circling the correct letter.

1. Grace Johnson used to live in _____b_____.

   a. San Diego   **b.** Sacramento   **c.** San Francisco

2. The house on 28th Avenue _____a_____ the house on Maple Street.

   a. isn't as expensive as   **b.** is as expensive as   **c.** is more expensive than

3. The house on 28th Avenue _____a_____ the house on Maple Street.

   a. has as many bedrooms as   **b.** doesn't have as many bedrooms as   **c.** has more bedrooms than

4. The house on Maple Street _____c_____ the house on 28th Avenue.

   a. has as many bathrooms as   **b.** doesn't have as many bathrooms as   **c.** has more bathrooms than

5. The house on 28th Avenue _____b_____ the house on Maple Street.

   a. is as convenient to public transportation as   **b.** isn't as convenient to public transportation as   **c.** is more convenient to public transportation than

6. Pets are allowed in _____c_____.

   a. both houses   **b.** the house on Maple Street   **c.** the house on 28th Avenue

In Your Own Words Tell a partner about a house you are familiar with. Use the chart as a guide. Use your own words. Say as much as you can.

Vocabulary
Places of Residence

Look at the pictures. Say each phrase.

a townhouse

an apartment complex

(continued on next page)

Building Materials

🎧 *Look at the pictures. Say each phrase.*

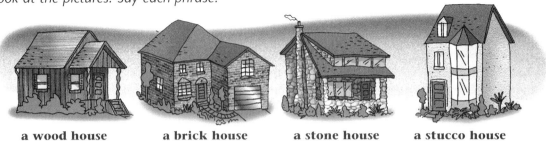

a wood house   **a brick house**   **a stone house**   **a stucco house**

Parts of a House

🎧 *Look at the picture. Say each word or phrase.*

the roof

the attic

the garden

the back door

the deck

upstairs

downstairs

the stairway

the basement

the garage

the porch

the gate

the front door

Vocabulary Practice

Study the vocabulary words again. Match each word or phrase with its definition.

1. a basement

2. a gate

3. brick

4. downstairs

5. an attic

6. a townhouse

7. wood

8. upstairs

9. a porch

10. a garden

a. the space or room at the top of a house

b. the lowest floor of a house, often underground

c. the part of a wall or a fence that opens

d. a building material in the shape of a rectangular block

e. a structure built around the front or back door of a house

f. on an upper floor

g. an area outside with plants or flowers

h. a house connected to other similar houses

i. on a lower floor

j. a building material that burns easily

▶ **Speaking**

Warm up: Talk about the picture with a partner. • Describe each house. • Compare the two houses. Which one is bigger? Which one would you rather have? • Talk about the people. What are they doing? Where do they work?

Then: Create conversations for the people. OR Tell a story. Say as much as you can.

FOR SALE

▶ **Writing:** An Advertisement

You are a realtor. Write an advertisement for your home or the home of a friend or a relative. Give as many details as you can.

If I were you, I'd speak to Glen first.

Warm up: A friend does something dishonest. What should you do? Say something or keep quiet? Read or listen. 🎧

Larry, I've got a real problem.

Oh yeah? What's wrong?

The other day my friend Glen—you know him—he's sort of short, with brown hair . . .

Uh-huh.

Well, he came into the store, and I sold him a $200 camera. On the way out, I saw him swipe a $90 lens.

What? Are you sure?

Positive. Now, if I tell my boss about Glen, I'll be betraying a friend.

On the other hand, if I mind my own business, I may end up being blamed for the missing lens. Either way, I lose.

Why do you suppose he did it?

Beats me. It can't be about money. He's loaded.

Comprehension: Inference and Interpretation

Complete each statement by circling the correct letter.

1. If Phil tells his boss about Glen, he will feel bad because _____.

   a. Glen is his friend   **b.** Glen is his boss's friend   **c.** Glen has his own business

2. If Phil doesn't tell his boss about Glen, he will worry that _____.

   a. he is hiding the truth   **b.** his boss might think he stole the lens   **c.** Glen will be angry

3. When Larry says, "No sense worrying now, Phil. You can cross that bridge when you come to it," he means _____.

   a. Glen probably didn't steal the lens   **b.** Phil and Glen should take a trip together   **c.** Phil can decide what to do after he speaks to Glen

Tell a partner what Phil saw in the store. Explain Phil's problem. Use your own words. Say as much as you can.

The present unreal conditional

Listening Focus • A Radio Show

Before You Listen: *Is it ever OK to copy someone's school work?*

🎧 *Listen to the radio call-in show, "If I Were You."*

IF I WERE YOU

ON AIR

Comprehension: Understanding Meaning from Context

🎧 *Listen to the radio call-in show again. Complete each statement by circling the correct letter.*

1. If Donna's boyfriend copied her paper, the teacher wouldn't know it was the same paper because _____.

   a. they have the same teacher   **b.** they have different teachers   **c.** they go to different schools

2. Al Steinberg says that if he were Donna, he would _____.

   a. let the boyfriend copy the paper   **b.** copy the paper but change it a little bit   **c.** not let the boyfriend copy the paper

3. Donna's boyfriend says that if he were in her position, he would _____.

   a. let her use his paper   **b.** not let her use his paper   **c.** help her write the paper

The Present Unreal Conditional

Use the present unreal conditional to talk about unreal, untrue, or imagined conditions and their results.

If Paul were rich, he would buy that camera. (Paul is not rich.)

Unreal conditional sentences have two clauses (parts): an *if*-clause and a result clause.

if-clause   result clause

If Lydia had a car, she would drive there.

Use the simple past tense form of the verb in the *if*-clause. Use **would, could,** or **might** in the result clause. The simple past tense form does *not* have past meaning. It can have present or future meaning.

if-clause   result clause

If I **had** enough money, I**'d buy** a new pair of skis. (I don't have enough money, so I won't buy new skis.)

Use **were** for all persons when the verb in the *if*-clause is a form of **be.**

Sarah would help you if she **were** here.

TIP: The result clause can be used alone.

A: What would you do if you found a suitcase filled with money?

B: *I'd give it to the police.*

GRAMMAR TASK: Find a present unreal conditional sentence and a real conditional sentence in the photo story on pages 50-51.

Grammar in a Context

Complete the present unreal conditional sentences. Use the correct form of the verbs.

Look, Tom. That's Noah driving his father's car. I'd better call his father. Noah doesn't have a license yet.

Calm down, Susan. It's none of your business. If I ___were___ you, I ___would___ my own business.
1. be   **2.** mind

If our kids ___took___ a drive in our car, I ___would want___ someone to let us know, wouldn't you?
3. take   **4.** want

Nope.

You can't be serious. Of course you would!

You know, Susan, if I ___had___ a dollar for every kid that ___drives___ before he ___gets___ his license, I ___would be___ a rich man.
5. have   **6.** drive   **7.** get   **8.** be

That doesn't make it right.

Grammar with a Partner

Choose a situation and have a brief conversation with a partner.
Use the present unreal conditional.

Example: **A:** What would you do if you found a gold ring in the bathroom of a restaurant?

   B: I'd give it to the manager.

1. You find a gold ring in the bathroom of a restaurant.

2. Your friend asks to see your answers to a test.

3. You see an old man stealing food from a supermarket.

4. Your best friend lies to you.

5. You don't like your friend's new boyfriend.

Heart to Heart

Reread the photo story on pages 50–51.
Then discuss with a partner what you
would do if you were Phil.

SOCIAL LANGUAGE 1

How To **respond to anger/persuade someone not to act impulsively**

Conversation

🎧 *Read and listen to the conversation.*

A: I've had it.

B: Calm down. What's the problem?

A: My boss. He's just awful. He never listens to me.

B: That's too bad.

A: I'm thinking of leaving.

B: Well, just don't do anything you might regret later.

A: Don't worry. I won't.

🎧 *Listen again and practice.*

Variations

Calm down.
Take it easy.
Relax.

Improvise

Have a conversation with a partner. One of you is very angry about something and wants to take action immediately. The other advises not acting impulsively. Use the conversation as a model. Use your own words.

Some Ideas

- A friend never returns your phone calls.
- A classmate copies your work.
- Your boss gives you too much work.
- Your husband or wife doesn't listen to you.
- A co-worker keeps interrupting your work.

or your OWN idea

☑ **Now you know how to respond to anger and persuade someone not to act impulsively.**

SOCIAL LANGUAGE 2

HOW TO empathize/suggest a course of action

Conversation

🎧 *Read and listen to the conversation.*

A: Did you hear about John?

B: No, what about him?

A: He lost his job.

B: Oh, that's terrible. He must be really <u>down</u>.

A: I know—I'd be very upset if I lost my job. Why don't we invite him out for dinner? That'll cheer him up.

B: Yeah, let's. It'll give him a chance to talk about it.

🎧 *Listen again and practice.*

Variations

down
down in the dumps
blue
miserable

Work with a partner. Something bad has happened to one of your friends. Tell your partner what happened. Discuss a way to help your friend feel better. Use the conversation as a model. Use your own words.

Some Ideas

- A friend lost a job.
- A friend had a fire in his house or apartment.
- A friend's car was stolen.
- A friend's spouse or girlfriend / boyfriend left him or her.

or your OWN idea

☑ **Now you know how to empathize and suggest a course of action.**

SOCIAL LANGUAGE 3

How to persuade someone not to do something

Conversation

🎧 *Read and listen to the conversation.*

A: Look at this ad: "Computers 70 percent off." I'm going to order one.

B: Sounds too good to be true. If I were you, I'd get more information before I gave them any money.

A: But the ad says, "Satisfaction Guaranteed."

B: Do you believe that?

🎧 *Listen again and practice.*

Bring in advertisements from magazines and newspapers. Improvise a conversation with a partner. You want to buy something you see in an ad. Your partner discourages you. Use the conversation as a model.

☑ **Now you know how to persuade someone not to do something.**

Authentic Reading

from The Associated Press

Before You Read: *Do you think most people in your town would return a wallet full of money that they found on the street?*

Read the article. 🎧

Best Place to Lose A Wallet Is Seattle

SEATTLE, Nov. 3 (AP)—If there is such a thing as a good place to lose your wallet, Seattle is it, an experiment by *Reader's Digest* has found.

The magazine left a trail of 120 "lost" wallets in 12 communities around the nation and kept track of how many were returned with the $50 contents intact: Seattle had the best rate of return, 9 of 10.

Despite the large role that chance could play in such a small experiment, Mayor Norm Rice of Seattle was ecstatic.

Three small cities were the next best, with a score of 8 in 10: Meadville, Pa.; Concord, N.H.; and Cheyenne, Wyo.

Of the two other big cities tested, St. Louis returned 7 in 10 and Atlanta trailed with 5 in 10, the magazine says in its December issue.

Source: The Associated Press

Comprehension: Understanding Meaning from Context

Read the article again. Circle the choice closest in meaning to each underlined word or phrase.

1. The magazine left a trail of 120 "lost" wallets in 12 communities around the nation and <u>kept track of</u> how many were returned with the $50 contents intact.

  a. recorded   **b.** didn't know   **c.** guessed

2. The magazine left a trail of 120 "lost" wallets in 12 communities around the nation and kept track of how many were returned with the $50 contents <u>intact</u>.

  a. missing   **b.** torn   **c.** not touched

3. Of the two other big cities tested, St. Louis returned 7 in 10 and Atlanta <u>trailed</u> with 5 in 10, the magazine says in its December issue.

  a. was last   **b.** was in the middle   **c.** was first

Talk with a partner. Compare your opinions.

"Finders keepers, losers weepers" is a well-known saying. It suggests that it is OK to keep what you find. What do you think of this idea? Is it OK to keep found property?

Listening with a Purpose

Determine Context

🎧 *Listen to the telephone conversations. Then complete each sentence in your own words.*

1. Marilee needs _____.

2. Marilee calls _____.

3. All of Marilee's friends _____.

Focus Attention

🎧 *Listen to the conversations again. Listen specifically for excuses. Then complete each sentence by circling the correct letter.*

1. Gretchen can't take care of Josh because _____.

    a. she gets nervous around small children   **b.** her parents are visiting her   **c.** she's going to be visiting her parents

2. Amy can't take care of Josh because _____.

    a. it's her day off   **b.** she's going on a trip this afternoon   **c.** she has to go to the airport

3. Jamie can't take care of Josh because _____.

    a. he has to play golf   **b.** he's working this afternoon   **c.** he's going to watch television

4. Stan can't take care of Josh because _____.

    a. he's cold   **b.** he doesn't feel well   **c.** he doesn't have anything to give to Josh

Bonus Listen to the conversations again. Listen specifically to what Marilee says. Find three additional ways to say "take care of."

    1. _____

    2. _____

    3. _____

Receptive Model

Some Ideas

- show me how this computer / fax machine / microwave works
- lend me your car for the afternoon
- give me a ride home
- watch my seat while I buy the newspaper
- watch my bags while I get something to eat
- take care of my cat while I'm on vacation

or your OWN *idea*

Form groups of five. One student makes a request. The others come up with excuses, using present unreal conditional sentences. Who can give the most unbelievable excuse?

Vocabulary

Honesty and Dishonesty

Say each word or phrase. Study the definitions.

---

the truth: The truth is something that is true.

> Karen said she was a magician. I didn't believe her, but it was the **truth**—she is a magician.

a lie: A lie is something you say that you know is not true.

> I told my boss I was sick, but that was a **lie**. I was really at the beach.

a white lie: A white lie is a small lie you tell when you don't want to hurt someone's feelings.

> Carter told Andrea he liked her hat. That was a **white lie**—he really didn't like it.

tell the truth: To tell the truth is to say something that you know is true.

> When I said that I couldn't dance, I was **telling the truth.**

lie: To lie is to say something that you know is not true. (To **lie** is to **tell a lie**.)

> I **lied** about what I did Friday night. I **told a lie** to my friend.

trust: To trust someone is to believe that that person will tell the truth and do the right thing.

> Natalie is always honest with me. I **trust** her completely.

(continued on next page)

> **honest:** An honest person tells the truth and tries to do the right thing.
>
> > Katrina is always **honest.** You can believe everything she says.
>
> **dishonest:** A dishonest person does not tell the truth and does not try to do the
> right thing.
>
> > I know Sal is **dishonest** because he's lied to me several times.

Vocabulary Practice

*Complete the following statements
with vocabulary words. Use each
word or phrase only once.
Use the correct verb form when
necessary.*

1. My friend Jared told me he had a college degree, but that was a _____.

I found out that he'd never gone to college.

2. My friend Christa told me she was going to Hawaii. At first I didn't believe her,

but I found out from her brother that it was the _____.

3. People in Seattle were more _____ than people in other cities. They

returned nine of the ten wallets that *Reader's Digest* "lost."

4. Bob got home at 4 A.M. Bob's father asked him what time he'd arrived home.

Bob _____. He said he'd gotten home at midnight.

5. I asked my friend if she liked my new haircut. She said she hated it.

She _____. At first I was angry, but later I was glad she was so honest.

6. Harriet tells me a lot of lies. I just can't _____ her.

7. Radio personality Al Steinberg told Donna it would be _____ to let her

boyfriend copy her paper.

8. Fran told her friend Julie a _____ when she said she liked Julie's new

dress. Actually, she didn't like the dress, but she didn't want to hurt Julie's feelings.

▶ **Speaking**

Warm up: Talk about the dinner party with a partner. • Talk about the food. Is it good or bad? • If you were a guest, what would you say about the food?

Then: Create conversations for the people. OR Tell a story. Say as much as you can.

▶ **Writing:** A Composition

Write about a time you told a lie or someone lied to you. Was there a good reason for the lie? What happened? Write as much as you can.

Review, SelfTest, and Extra Practice

Units 1-5

Part 1

Review

Our Top Story: A Happy Ending

🎧 *Listen to the TV news broadcast.*

LAKEWOOD'S population increase: 14% in the last 6 years.

SelfTest

Comprehension: Factual Recall

🎧 *Listen to the news broadcast again. Then complete each sentence by circling the correct letter.*

1. The kidnapped baby was _____ old.

   a. three months   **b.** three weeks   **c.** three days

2. The _____ of Sandra Elsworth, the woman charged with the crime, called police and told them where the child was.

   a. daughter   **b.** sister   **c.** mother

3. The population of Lakewood has grown by about _____ people in the last six years.

   a. 43,000   **b.** 4,300   **c.** 14,300

4. The city of Lakewood has bought old houses and is selling them for _____ each.

   a. $10,000   **b.** $1,000   **c.** $100,000

5. According to health officials, the greatest food-related health danger now comes from _____.

   a. food served at fast-food restaurants   **b.** people not washing their hands after preparing food at home   **c.** restaurant workers not washing their hands

6. Effective immediately, all those wishing to see movies that are rated as violent will have to _____.

   a. go to movies with their parents   **b.** have a driver's license   **c.** show identification to prove their age

Comprehension: Verb Form Review

🎧 *Listen to the news broadcast again. Then complete the following sentences with correct verb forms.*

1. The child _____ _____ from Lakewood General Hospital on Saturday night by a woman claiming to be a doctor.

2. Elsworth's brother told KNZX reporters that his sister _____ _____ _____ from mental problems for the last three years.

3. Does it seem to you that there are more people in Lakewood than there _____ _____ _____?

4. In the same time period, the population of rural areas _____ _____ _____.

5. The mayor said, "_____ _____ one of these houses if I _____ already _____ a house of my own."

6. Sounds like a pretty good deal, _____ it, Lisa?

7. Local health officials say that fast-food restaurants _____ now _____ the safest places to eat.

8. This policy _____ _____ for many years but _____ never _____ seriously _____.

Heart to **Heart**

Talk with a partner about one or more of the news stories on pages 62–63. Then read the ideas at the right. What would you do? Compare your opinions.

Extra Practice

Some Ideas

- If a relative of yours did something illegal, would you call the police?
- If you were the mayor of your town, what would you do to improve your area?
- Do you think that people under the age of eighteen should not be able to attend certain movies? Why or why not?

Grammar with a Partner

A. Work with a partner. Look at the pictures. Compare Lakewood in the past and Lakewood today. Use the expressions below or your own ideas. Practice **used to**.

Lakewood in the Past   **Lakewood Today**

live on farms   grow their own vegetables
live in the city / in apartments   shop at supermarkets

ride in buggies   make their own clothes
ride in cars   buy clothes in stores

Example: People used to live on farms. Today they live . . .

B. Now give your opinion. Use the following expressions or your own ideas to compare Lakewood in the past and Lakewood today. Use **not as.**

families / large   life / easy
clothing / comfortable   life / interesting

Example: Families today aren't as large as they were in the past.

Letters to the Editor

🎧 *Read or listen to the letters to the editor of a newspaper.*

Editor, *The Times*

Three Cheers for the Theater Owners

Hip, hip, hooray! For years now, many of us parents have been asking theater owners not to let kids into adult movies. Until now, though, they've ignored our requests. From now on, young people will have to prove they're eighteen to be admitted into any adult movie. There will be no exceptions. That's the way it should be.

Kids are influenced by what they see on TV and in the movies. If they see violence on a TV or movie screen, there's a better chance that they'll be violent.

I know some people say that if parents don't want their children to see certain movies, they should simply tell their kids they can't see them. But now that in most families mothers and fathers both have to work full-time, parents can't supervise their children all the time. Everybody has to help out. There have to be laws. We have to enforce them.

Thank you, theater owners. You've finally done something intelligent.

Kevin Clark, Lakewood
October 13

Editor, *The Times*

Theater Owners Are All Wet

I think the new plan to keep young people out of "adult" movies is ridiculous. Teenagers understand the world. They're not children.

Some people say that when teenagers see violent movies, they get violent. Maybe that's true for one teenager out of a thousand. Wouldn't it also be true for adults?

The theater owners' new policy is another example of censorship. If the policy goes into effect, we will lose our freedom to choose the movies we see. In my history class, we're studying the damage censorship can cause. People should be able to make their own decisions. I hope the theater owners change their minds.

Heather Friendly, Lakewood
October 12
via e-mail

SelfTest

Comprehension: Understanding Meaning from Context

Circle the choice closest in meaning to each underlined word or phrase.

1. <u>Three cheers for the theater owners</u>.
   - a. I disagree with the theater owners.
   - b. I agree with the theater owners.
   - c. The theater owners are good businesspeople.

2. Until now, though, <u>they've ignored our requests</u>.
   - a. they've done what we've asked
   - b. they don't understand what we've asked
   - c. they haven't done what we've asked

3. Parents can't <u>supervise</u> their children all the time.
   - a. be in charge of
   - b. punish
   - c. understand

4. There have to be laws. We have to <u>enforce them</u>.
   - a. understand them
   - b. write them
   - c. make people obey them

5. Theater owners are <u>all wet</u>.
   - a. right
   - b. wrong
   - c. angry

6. The theater owners' new policy is another example of <u>censorship</u>.
   - a. giving people new freedoms
   - b. making new laws
   - c. taking freedoms away from people

Comprehension: Inference and Interpretation

Read the letters again. Then complete each sentence by circling the correct letter.

1. The writer of the first letter thinks that seeing violent movies _____ make teenagers violent.
   - a. can't
   - b. won't
   - c. may

2. The writer of the second letter thinks that seeing violent movies _____ make most teenagers violent.
   - a. will
   - b. could
   - c. won't

3. The writer of the second letter _____ a teenager.
   - a. is probably
   - b. probably isn't
   - c. isn't

Heart to Heart

Extra Practice

Talk with a partner. Compare your opinions.

Do you think seeing violent movies makes people violent?

Should teenagers be allowed to see any movies they want?

Which letter on page 66 do you agree with more?

Writing

Extra Practice

Write your own letter to the editor of a newspaper. Choose one of these topics or another topic that interests you.

All people should be allowed to see any movie they want.
Teenagers shouldn't be allowed to see adult movies.

Use the letters on page 66 as a model.

Part 3

Review

Advertisements

🎧 *Listen to the advertisements.*

SelfTest

Comprehension: Confirming Content

🎧 *Listen to the advertisements again. Match each ad with the correct product.*

1. Ad number 1 is for _____.   clothes

2. Ad number 2 is for _____.   cars

3. Ad number 3 is for _____.   soap

4. Ad number 4 is for _____.   chocolate pies

Comprehension: Factual Recall

🎧 *Now listen once more. Match each ad with the correct place.*

1. Ad number 1: _____

2. Ad number 2: _____

3. Ad number 3: _____

4. Ad number 4: _____

Nickels

Thompson's Autos

Kringles Supermarket

Gracy's Department Store

Extra Practice

Writing

🎧 *Listen to the ads again. Then write your own ad. Use the listening as a model.*

Some Ideas

- a clothing sale
- a new movie
- a luxury hotel
- a new restaurant
- an electronics sale
- a concert

or **your OWN** idea

SOCIAL LANGUAGE Review

Review 1

🎧 *Read and listen to the conversation.*

(continued on next page)

Work with a partner. The two of you meet in a video store, bookstore, or music store. You are looking for a video, book, or CD.

Your partner makes a suggestion and then suggests that you do something together. Use the conversation as a model.

Review 2

🎧 *Read and listen to the conversation.*

A: I love your car. How long have you had it?

B: About a year.

A: How do you feel about driving such a big car?

B: It's OK. Why? Are you thinking of buying one?

A: I may buy one, or I may lease one. My old one was stolen last month.

B: Oh, that's terrible. If I were you, I'd buy. And I'd get a small car. You'll save on gas and you won't have trouble parking.

A: That's what I'll probably do. One thing I do know—I've had it with buses. They're always late and they take forever.

Work with a partner. Ask about something your partner has and you are considering getting—for example, a watch, a car, a computer, or an apartment. Your partner gives an opinion and makes a suggestion. Use the conversation as a model.

SOCIAL LANGUAGE SelfTest

Circle the appropriate statement or question to complete each of the following conversations.

1. A: Are you getting something to drink?

   B: _____

   a. Yes. Would you mind watching my bags?

   b. Yes. I don't mind drinking.

   c. Yes. Not at all.

2. A: _____

   B: Yes. I didn't like it much, though.

   a. Did you like working there?

   b. Didn't you use to work at Sloan's?

   c. Do you like it better?

3. A: Do you know anything about the Hunan Balcony restaurant?

   B: _____

   a. It's supposed to be good.

   b. Yes, I know.

   c. Who knows?

4. A: I've had it.

   B: _____

   a. Take it easy.

   b. What do you have?

   c. That's easy.

5. A: _____

   B: I don't think so.

   a. How do you feel about walking on the grass?

   b. Are you sure?

   c. Are you allowed to walk on the grass?

6. A: I'm thinking of leaving the company.

   B: _____

   a. Don't do anything you might regret later.

   b. Are you having a lot of guests?

   c. Do you like it better?

7. A: How do you feel about murder mysteries?

   B: _____

   a. It depends on the mystery.

   b. I feel good.

   c. I'd rather not.

8. A: _____

   B: Really? Why would she do that?

   a. Is Jennifer quitting?

   b. Why won't Jennifer quit?

   c. I heard Jennifer's quitting.

9. A: I've been trying to find a good restaurant.

   B: _____

   a. Have you tried Arturo's?

   b. Not at all.

   c. Do you have a good restaurant?

10. A: How's your new dentist?

   B: _____

   a. He must be really down.

   b. Fine, thanks.

   c. I think he's excellent.

I wonder if she forgot about the party.

Warm up: Does time mean something different to different people? Can you give an example? Listen. 🎧

Comprehension: Understanding Meaning from Context

🎧 *Listen to the conversation again. Match each underlined phrase with its meaning.*

1. Allie will be here <u>any minute</u>.

a. going to

2. Allie will be here any minute. <u>Take my word for it.</u>

b. Get in the car.

3. Hi, Anna. <u>Hop in.</u>

c. very soon

4. Sonya was <u>about to</u> call the police.

d. Believe me.

Listen to the conversation again. Tell your partner about Sonya. What are her worries? What happens? Use your own words. Say as much as you can.

Embedded questions

Reading Focus • A Magazine Article

Before You Read: What is culture? How are people from different cultures different? How are they the same?

Read the article. (Note the examples of embedded questions in bold type.) 🎧

CROSSWINDS

Not Too Close!

by Portia Squires

Jeff is at his company's international sales meeting, and there are people from a lot of different countries. Tonight is the welcome party. Jeff has just gotten himself something to eat when Simon, a young man from another country, engages him in conversation. Jeff is interested in what Simon has to say. Before long, however, he starts to feel a bit uncomfortable. He wonders **why Simon is standing so close to him**. He doesn't want to offend him, though, so he starts to back up, very slowly. But each time he backs up, Simon moves forward, and then Jeff moves backward again. Jeff gets more and more uncomfortable and frustrated. He doesn't know **how he should respond**. He starts to think that Simon is aggressive and pushy.

Meanwhile, Simon is feeling some frustration and discomfort of his own. He thinks Jeff is congenial and finds him an interesting conversationalist, but he can't understand **why Jeff keeps moving away from him**. Simon even wonders **if he might have bad breath**. Actually, Simon is not so much uncomfortable as he is

puzzled. He is enjoying the conversation but can't understand **why Jeff seems cold and unfriendly**. Soon Jeff excuses himself and leaves. Both men feel dissatisfied with the conversation. They don't understand **what went wrong.**

Anthropologist Edward T. Hall has given us a clear explanation of the kind of problem Jeff and Simon are having. Different cultures, Hall says, have different definitions of space. In each culture, there is an imaginary "bubble" of space around the individual members of that culture. If it's a small bubble, other people can come quite close. If it's a big bubble, other people shouldn't come too close. The problem in cross-cultural encounters lies in our not knowing **what the rules of other cultures are**. We can't assume that our cultural ways are "right" and the ways of other cultures are "wrong."

The world is becoming more and more globalized. That doesn't mean, however, that cultural differences are becoming less important. If anything, it means that we all need to become more sensitive to cultural differences.

Comprehension: Inference and Interpretation

Now discuss the following possible conclusions with a partner. Explain your opinions.

1. Jeff is cold and unfriendly.

2. Simon is aggressive and pushy.

3. Cultural differences will continue to be important in the future.

Embedded Questions

An embedded question is a question inside a larger sentence.

question	embedded question
Did Allie forget about the party?	I wonder *if Allie forgot about the party.*
Where is Allie?	I don't know *where Allie is.*

Embedded *yes-no* questions use *if, whether,* or *whether or not.* Their meanings are similar.

question	embedded *yes-no* question
Is she coming?	Do you know *if she's coming?*
	OR
	Do you know *whether she's coming?*
Has she left?	Do you know *whether or not she's left?*

An embedded question does not use question word order. If an embedded question is in a statement, use a period. If it is in a question, use a question mark.

question	embedded *wh-* question
What time is the party?	Do you know *what time the party is?*
	NOT: ~~Do you know what time is the party~~ ?
Where did she go?	I wonder *where she went.* (a statement)

▼ **GRAMMAR TASK:** Find three embedded questions in "Not Too Close!" on page 74. Change them to real questions.

Example: He wonders why Simon is standing so close to him. → Why is Simon standing so close to him?

Grammar in a Context

Complete the conversation. Change the indicated questions to embedded questions.
*(The meanings of **if, whether,** and **whether or not** are similar. You can use them all.)*

Look, there's Laila Preston, our old neighbor. She got a job in Summit, didn't she?

Yeah. I wonder _____.
1. What is she doing now?

Something with computers, I think. I wonder _____
2. How do she and
_____.
Roger like their new neighbors?

(continued on next page)

Hi, Laila. How're you doing?

Fine. You both look great.

You, too. Any good buys?

Not today. . . . Well, I've got to run. It was really good seeing you two. We'll have to get together sometime.

I wonder _____.
3. Did she mean it?

Meant what?

I wonder _____.
4. Does she really want to get together? Since they moved, we haven't seen them once.

Let's find out _____.
5. Do they want to see us?
Call her tonight. Invite them for dinner next Friday.

Good idea. I will.

Grammar with a Partner

Bring a magazine or newspaper photo of people to class. Ask a partner questions about each photo. Begin with "Do you know . . . ?"

Example: Do you know who the people in the photo are?

Some Ideas

- Who are they?
- Is she married?
- Where was the photo taken?
- When was the photo taken?
- What does she do?

or your OWN idea

SOCIAL LANGUAGE 1

HOW TO ask about someone's identity/offer an explanation

Conversation

🎧 *Read and listen to the conversation.*

A: John, you see that man over there?

B: You mean the one next to Marcus?

A: Yeah. Do you know what his name is?

B: Sure. That's Zeb Richards.

A: Oh. That's right. Do you know what he does?

B: He's a movie director.

A: Oh, that explains why he knows so much about movies.

🎧 *Listen again and practice.*

Variations

that explains why
no wonder
now I understand why

Ask your partner about someone. Your partner gives you information about that person. Use the conversation as a model.

Some Ideas

- People are taking his (or her) picture.
- People are asking him (or her) questions.
- People are getting his (or her) autograph.
- He (or she) knows so much about food / the law / music, etc.

or your OWN idea

☑ **Now you know how to ask about someone's identity. You also know how to offer an explanation.**

SOCIAL LANGUAGE 2

How TO ask for and make a suggestion

Conversation

🎧 *Read and listen to the conversation.*

A: Todd's family invited me to dinner. I have no idea what to bring.

B: Well . . . flowers are always nice.

A: Good idea. Are there any flower shops around here?

B: There's one between Market and Elm Streets. Do you know where that is?

A: Oh yeah. I'm pretty sure I do. Thanks.

🎧 *Listen again and practice.*

First make a list of as many gifts as you can. Then work with a partner. You were invited to a dinner, a wedding, a birthday, or a graduation. You don't know what to take. Your partner makes a suggestion. Use the conversation as a model.

☑ **Now you know how to ask for and make a suggestion.**

HOW TO **offer and accept help/reassure someone**

Conversation

🎧 *Read and listen to the conversation.*

A: Do you need a lift home?

B: It's nice of you to offer, but I can manage.

A: It's no trouble at all. Really.

B: Well, if that's the case, I'd appreciate it.

🎧 *Listen again and practice.*

Improvise a conversation with a partner. One of you offers help in some way. The other first refuses and then accepts the offer. Use the conversation as a model.

Some Ideas

- a ride home
- some help serving or cooking a meal
- some help moving something heavy
- some help operating a computer, fax machine, or VCR

or your OWN idea

☑ **Now you know how to offer and accept help and how to reassure someone.**

Receptive Model

Authentic Reading

from the Internet

***B**efore You Read: Think about a time someone was rude to you. What did the person do? How did you respond?*

Read these excerpts from "Global Village Etiquette." 🎧

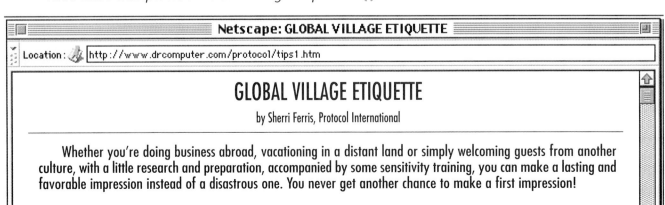

Netscape: GLOBAL VILLAGE ETIQUETTE

Location: http://www.drcomputer.com/protocol/tips1.htm

GLOBAL VILLAGE ETIQUETTE

by Sherri Ferris, Protocol International

Whether you're doing business abroad, vacationing in a distant land or simply welcoming guests from another culture, with a little research and preparation, accompanied by some sensitivity training, you can make a lasting and favorable impression instead of a disastrous one. You never get another chance to make a first impression!

Here are rules on social interaction to keep in mind:

- Be patient when building trust in establishing relationships. People from other countries take much longer than Americans and observe greater formality than we do. You wouldn't want to ask someone from Great Britain his or her occupation on first meeting.

- It is courteous to ALWAYS stand when you are introduced to another human being—no matter the culture.

- Slow down your speech and don't raise your voice because you think someone cannot understand you. Have you noticed how people just talk louder to be understood? Volume doesn't usually increase comprehension. People with foreign accents are not necessarily hard of hearing.

- Non-verbal interaction cues are extremely important. "Yes" or an affirmative nod often means "yes I hear you" in Asian cultures, not "yes, I agree." By looking at the interaction through American eyes, you might think you just closed the deal of the century. You must understand that by avoiding the word "no," some Asians believe they can avoid creating any disharmony, and harmony is a cherished value in this culture.

- Never slap someone's back, the "good old Joe" American routine. Touching and rules of social distance vary in other cultures.

| Back | Etiquette Tip II | Etiquette Tip III |

Source: Protocol International, 2040 Polk Street #164, San Francisco, CA 94109, http://www.drcomputer.com/protocol/tips1.htm
E-mail: ProtIntl@ix.netcom.com

Comprehension: Factual Recall

*Read "Global Village Etiquette" again. Then mark the following statements **T** (true) or **F** (false).*

1. _____ Americans are as formal as people from other countries.

2. _____ After you are introduced to a person from Great Britain, it is a good idea to ask, "What do you do?"

3. _____ The author suggests standing when introduced.

4. _____ If you think a person can't understand you, speak louder.

5. _____ When some people nod, they may mean that they hear you, not that they agree with you.

6. _____ Some people may not like a friendly slap on the back.

*Think about your own culture and decide if the writer gave good advice. Write **agree** or **disagree** next to each suggestion in the reading. Then talk with a partner. Compare your opinions.*

 *(reinforces offering an explanation)*

Look at the list. Check whether you think each action is acceptable or unacceptable.

	Acceptable	Unacceptable
Clapping your hands to signal a waiter	☐	☐
Cutting into a line	☐	☐
Arriving late for a party	☐	☐
Arriving late for a business meeting	☐	☐
Hugging people when you first meet them	☐	☐
Asking someone's age	☐	☐
Asking someone's weight	☐	☐
Asking if someone is married	☐	☐
Kissing relatives at an airport	☐	☐

Now, with a partner, choose one of the behaviors that is unacceptable. Explain why.
What should you do instead? Present your explanation to the class.

Pronunciation

Prefixes

Prefixes are usually unstressed. Therefore, they may be difficult to hear.
Listen to the sentences.

1. In my opinion, he's <u>irresponsible</u>.
In my opinion, he's <u>responsible</u>.

2. I'm <u>uncomfortable</u> in large groups.
I'm <u>comfortable</u> in large groups.

3. That plan is <u>impractical</u>.
That plan is <u>practical</u>.

4. Is it <u>illegal</u> to park here?
Is it <u>legal</u> to park here?

5. That young woman is very <u>independent</u>.
That young woman is very <u>dependent</u>.

6. That's an <u>uncommon</u> name.
That's a <u>common</u> name.

Listen again and repeat.

Listening with a Purpose

Focus Attention

🎧 *Listen to the conversation about customs and manners.*

🎧 *Now listen to the conversation again. The people ask a number of questions.*
Listen specifically for the questions. Then complete each sentence by circling the correct letter.

1. The male speaker asks Marcos _____.

    a. how long he has been in the United States
    b. how he likes the United States

2. Marcos asks _____.

    a. how much you should leave as a tip in a restaurant
    b. if you should leave a tip in a restaurant

3. Marcos asks _____.

    a. what you should bring for the host of a party
    b. if you should bring something for the host of a party

4. Marcos asks _____.

    a. if it's wrong to open a door for a woman
    b. if women like to open doors for themselves

5. Marcos asks _____.

    a. if you're supposed to shake hands with a woman when you meet her
    b. if you're supposed to kiss a woman on the cheek when you meet her

 **Listen to the conversation again. Then, in your own words, tell a partner about some social customs in North America. Compare them with customs in other places you know.** 🎧

Vocabulary

Polite and Impolite

🎧 *Say each word or phrase. Study the definitions.*

---

body language: Body language is the way you move or position your body that shows what you are feeling or thinking.

    I could tell by her **body language** that she didn't enjoy talking to me.

personal space: Personal space is the physical space you feel comfortable keeping between yourself and others.

    Don't stand too close to Liz. She needs her **personal space.**

(continued on next page)

a territory: A territory is a specific place or area that a person or group owns.

Richie's room is his **territory**—no one enters without his permission.

behavior: Your behavior is the way you say or do things.

Jesse's **behavior** has improved tremendously this year.

privacy: To have privacy is to be able to be alone.

Leave me alone; I need **privacy** right now.

belong: When something belongs to you, you own it.

That briefcase **belongs** to me. See, it has my name on it.

gesture: To gesture is to use your arms, hands, or head to indicate or "say" something.

Darnell **gestures** a lot when he speaks.

invade: To invade a place or space is to enter it without permission.

Don't **invade** Felicia's space; she can get very angry.

rude: Someone who speaks or acts in a way that is not polite is rude.

Frank is very **rude.** He's always interrupting me.

Vocabulary Practice

Look at the picture. Then complete the following paragraph with vocabulary words. Use the correct form of verbs.

Mrs. Branford has been sitting on this park bench for more than half an hour, eating her lunch and reading her newspaper. The problem is, these young men have just come along and have _____ her personal space. One of

1.

the men has picked up her newspaper. He doesn't realize that it _____ to

2.

Mrs. Branford. He hasn't asked her permission. She thinks their _____ is

3.

very _____. She's tried to show her anger through her _____,

4.   **5.**

but neither man is paying any attention. Right now one of the men is holding her

newspaper and is _____ to the other man. Mrs. Branford wants the two men

6.

to go away. She wants _____.

7.

▶ **Speaking**

Warm up: Talk about the picture with a partner. • Ask your partner embedded questions about this picture—for example, "I wonder where the two women are going." • Talk about the people in the picture. • Who is polite? Who is impolite? Why?

Then: Create conversations for the people. OR Tell a story. Say as much as you can.

▶ **Writing:** A Composition

Look back at "Global Village Etiquette" on pages 78–79. Then write a composition about the correct behavior for people of your age in your community. Mention at least three things that visitors should or shouldn't do. Explain why the behavior is acceptable or unacceptable.

We must be close to the top by now.

Receptive Model

Warm up: *When you travel, do you prefer guided tours or traveling on your own? Read or listen.* 🎧

OK. Who's coming along?

Count me out. I'm still beat from yesterday's adventure.

Me, too. I'll pass. I prefer guided tours, anyway. I think there might be one at noon.

What about you, Amber?

Sure. I like exploring on my own better than with a whole group of people. How far is it to the top?

Oh, pretty far—it'll take at least a couple of hours.

Later

Are we almost there?

Just a little bit farther. Here. Have some water.

The first rule of hiking: You absolutely must not get dehydrated.

Thanks. We must be close to the top by now. Are you sure you know the way?

Of course. Anyway, half the fun is finding it.

I guess so.

84   UNIT 7

I can't go on, Jessica. Go on without me.

No way. I'm not leaving you behind. You're not a quitter.

You can make it. Come on, Am.

Thirty minutes later

We made it. Now aren't you glad you stuck with it? . . .

I can't believe this place. It's fantastic. No wonder they call this Paradise Peak.

Comprehension: Understanding Meaning from Context

Circle the choice closest in meaning to each underlined word or phrase.

1. <u>Count me out</u>.

　a. I'm not going.　　**b.** I'm going.　　**c.** I'm not counting.

2. <u>I'm still beat from yesterday's adventure</u>.

　a. I had a fight yesterday.　**b.** I'm tired from what we did yesterday.　**c.** I really enjoyed what we did yesterday.

3. You're not a <u>quitter</u>.

　a. person who doesn't finish what he or she starts　**b.** person who is lazy　**c.** person who doesn't know when to stop

4. Now aren't you glad you <u>stuck with it</u>?

　a. continued　　**b.** left　　**c.** stayed at the hotel

5. No wonder they call this <u>Paradise</u> Peak.

　a. a high place　　**b.** a beautiful place　　**c.** an imaginary place

Talk about the photo story with a partner. Tell your partner about the people. What happens in the story? Use your own words. Say as much as you can.

Must, might, **and can't**

Listening Focus • A Conversation

Before You Listen: *Think about one of the best vacations you've had. Where did you go?*

🎧 *Listen to the conversation between two people on a tour bus.*

Comprehension: Inference and Interpretation

🎧 *Listen to the conversation again. Listen to the guesses each person makes. Then complete each statement by circling the correct letter.*

1. When Caroline says, "We might be in Belgium," she means that _____.

    a. she's sure they're in Belgium

    b. she's almost sure they're in Belgium

    c. she thinks it's possible they're in Belgium

2. When Stuart says, "This can't be France," he means that _____.

    a. they probably aren't in France

    b. it's possible they're in France

    c. it's impossible that they're in France

3. When Stuart says, "This must be Belgium," he means that _____.

    a. he's sure they're in Belgium

    b. he's almost sure they're in Belgium

    c. it's possible they're in Belgium

4. The season must be _____.

    a. late spring

    b. midsummer

    c. winter

Why don't Stuart and Caroline know where they are? Tell a partner. Use your own words.

Talk with a partner. Compare your opinions.

What are the advantages of going on a guided tour? What are the disadvantages?

Must, Might, and Can't

A logical guess based on facts is a conclusion. Use *must, might,* or *can't* to state conclusions.

Use *must* if you are almost sure.

> **A:** I haven't eaten since yesterday. (fact)
> **B:** You *must* be hungry. (conclusion)

Use *may* or *might* if you conclude something is possible but you aren't sure.

> **A:** Corrine isn't in class today. (fact)
> **B:** She *may* be sick. Or she *might* be out of town. (conclusions)

Use *can't* if you conclude that something is impossible.

> **A:** Isn't Donald in Hawaii?
> **B:** I saw him this morning. (fact)
> He *can't* be in Hawaii. (conclusion)

TIP: When we use *must* or *might* to make a negative conclusion, we usually don't contract.
I sent Noah a letter to this address, but it came back. He *must not* live there anymore.
(NOT: ~~He mustn't live there anymore.~~)

GRAMMAR TASK: There are two sentences with *must* in the photo story on pages 84–85.
Find the one that states a conclusion.

Grammar in a Context

*Where does Charlotte live? Read the facts and state your conclusions. Use **must, might,** and **can't**.*

Fact 1: Charlotte lives in Europe.

Fact 2: She lives near the Atlantic Ocean.

Fact 3: People in her country speak Spanish.

1. She _____ live in France.

3. She _____ live in Portugal.

5. She _____ live in England.

2. She _____ live in Mexico.

4. She _____ live in Poland.

6. She _____ live in Spain.

Must and Should

You can also use *must* for obligation. *Must* is similar in meaning to *have to* and *have got to.*
Must not for obligation can be contracted to *mustn't.*

> In many countries, you *must* be at least eighteen to get a driver's license. (You can't get a license if you aren't eighteen.)

Use *should* to show that something is advisable but is not an obligation.

> You *should* take a credit card with you on a trip, in case of emergency. (It's advisable—a good idea—but it's not an obligation.)

Must and *should* don't have *-s* in the third-person singular. They are followed by the base form.

GRAMMAR TASK: Find the sentence with *must* for obligation in the photo story on pages 84–85. Say it another way.

Grammar in a Context

*Use **must** or **should** to complete the passage.*

Travel Abroad

You _____must_____ have a valid passport to enter most countries. To get a passport, you

1.

_____must_____ bring to the passport office proof of citizenship: either a birth certificate,

2.

a naturalization certificate, or a previous passport.

Not all countries require identification for entry, but you _____should_____ still bring

3.

along a driver's license, a credit card, or your military papers, just to be safe.

We recommend that you be careful when traveling. You _____should_____

4.

keep your passport in a safe place like a pouch or a money belt. You

_____must_____ not leave it lying around in your hotel room.

5.

SOCIAL LANGUAGE 1

HOW TO **state possibilities/express irritation**

Conversation

🎧 *Read and listen to the conversation.*

A: Any idea where Joe is?

B: He might be at work.

A: At this hour?

B: It's possible. He mentioned something about a special project.

A: I can't believe that guy. He's never around when you want him.

🎧 *Listen again and practice.*

Work with a partner. You are trying to find someone. Your partner makes guesses about where the person might be. Use the conversation as a model.

☑ **Now you know how to state possibilities and express irritation.**

HOW TO express obligations/draw conclusions

Conversation

🎧 *Read and listen to the conversation.*

A: Are you going to the club?

B: No. I've got to pack.

A: For what?

B: Well, I'm going to Tahiti in the morning.

A: Tahiti? You must be really excited.

B: I am. I can't wait.

🎧 *Listen again and practice.*

HOW TO give surprising information/express surprise

Conversation

🎧 *Read and listen to the conversation.*

A: Guess where Grandma and Grandpa are going on vacation.

B: I give up. Where?

A: Camping in Alberta.

B: Camping? You must be kidding.

A: No, really. They wanted a change from those five-star hotels.

B: Well, they'll get it.

🎧 *Listen again and practice.*

Variations

You must be kidding.
You can't be serious.
You must be joking.
You can't mean that.

Improvise

Improvise a conversation with a partner. Talk about unusual travel plans. Get as much information as you can about the trip. Use the conversations as models.

☑ **Now you know how to draw conclusions. You also know how to give surprising information and express surprise.**

Inter-Action *(reinforces **must, might,** and **can't**)*

Look at these pictures. With a partner, make conclusions about where they might be.

Example: This might be in Europe. It might be in Greece or Turkey.

1.

2.

3.

4.

*Then turn your book upside down for the names of the places. Use **must** to decide which place is which.*

Answers: Anasazi Indian cliff dwellings in Mesa Verde, Colorado, United States; Angkor Wat, Cambodia; Pyramids of Giza, Egypt; The Acropolis in Athens, Greece.

Would you like to visit any of these places? If you visited one of these sites, what would you like to do?

Authentic Reading

from *Consumer Reports*

Before You Read: What time of year do you usually travel? Are crowds a problem at those times?

Read the article.

A hermit's guide to Yellowstone
Getting away from them all

Yellowstone National Park covers 3400 square miles, 99 percent of them undeveloped, yet about one-fourth of our readers who visited said the park was too crowded. It was too crowded for two reasons: Most people go at the same time, and most people go to the same places. Last year, for example, three million people visited this grandfather of all parks—and more than half went in July and August. Here are strategies to help you beat the crowds. The tactics apply not only to *Yellowstone,* but to many popular sites.

Go off-season. You'll feel less stress and will put less stress on the area itself. "We should be using the shoulder seasons, if we can," says outgoing Park Service director Roger Kennedy. About one in three readers who saw *Yellowstone* in June, July, or August said it was too crowded, whereas only about one in seven who went in other months felt that way. Delaying even a month can make a big difference: About half as many people went to *Yellowstone* last September as went in

August. For a different experience, you can visit in winter, when the roads are groomed for snowmobile and snow-bus travel. *Yellowstone* has about one-fortieth as many visitors in December as in July.

Get off the beaten path. As long as you're in the neighborhood, you'll probably want to take the road most traveled, to Old Faithful, the famous geyser that erupts every 65 minutes or so, and the park's other premier attractions. But park roads can take you only so far. *Yellowstone* has 1000 miles of trails; rangers can recommend those that match your fitness level and time limitations. Walk, and you'll leave most people behind: 19 percent of our readers didn't hike or walk at all in the site they visited; of the hikers, 40 percent walked a mile or less.

Comprehension: Drawing Conclusions

*A. Read these conclusions based on the article. Then mark each sentence **T** (true) or **F** (false).*

1. _____ Yellowstone must be big.

2. _____ Most people must want to visit Yellowstone in the winter.

3. _____ Yellowstone must be very crowded in the summer.

4. _____ Yellowstone must have a variety of hiking trails.

B. *Put a check next to the pieces of advice that are based on the article.*

1. _____ You shouldn't visit Yellowstone in July.

2. _____ You shouldn't visit Old Faithful. It's too crowded.

3. _____ You should ask rangers for advice about trails.

4. _____ You shouldn't walk along the trails without a guide. They're too dangerous.

Travel Adventure

*(reinforces **might** and **must**)*

Play in pairs. Take turns. Toss a coin to move. One side of the coin lets you move ahead one space. The other side lets you move two.

*When you land on a space with a clue, say where you might be or must be. Get one point for a correct **might** answer, and two points for a correct **must** answer. Go back one space for a wrong answer.*

Answers are on page 142.

Example: You're in a country where people speak Spanish.
"I might be in Peru." (You get one point.)

1 START	2 You're on a train that crosses the Danube River.	3 After you cross the Danube, you see a sign that says "Buda 1 km, Pest 3 km."	4	5 You hear people speaking a language that you're sure is Italian.
10 COUNTRIES **TOURIST TRAP! LOSE TWO TURNS.**	9 A sign by the side of the road says "Koalas have the right of way."	8 You fly to a new country. You land at an airport and buy something. It costs two dollars.	7	6 A road sign says "Bern 5 km."
11	12 You see several pyramids.	13 You hear people speaking Spanish, and a sign says "Yucatán."	14	15 Добро Пожаловать You see a sign written in Cyrillic.
20 **FINISH**	19 You see a tall mountain and near it a big hotel named Hotel Kilimanjaro.	18 You hear people speaking, and someone says the language is Swahili.	17	16 You find yourself in a place called Red Square.

Listening with a Purpose

Listening Between the Lines

🎧 Listen to the conversation on a train.

🎧 Now listen again and complete the conclusions the speakers draw.

1. No. But it must be the _____ for Brighton. I think it's the only one that leaves at 3:00.

2. No, really. It must be _____.

3. He _____ be Elvis.

4. You must think _____.

5. Judging from your accent, I'd say you girls must be from _____.

6. Manchester? Oh, no! This must not be the _____.

🎧 Now listen between the lines for the reasons each speaker comes to the conclusions above.

Example: Jane and Nadia think they are going to Brighton because there is only one train at that time.

 **Tell a partner what happened on the train. Use your own words. Say as much as you can.**

Vocabulary

Common Phrasal Verbs

🎧 Look at the pictures. Say each phrase.

get along
They don't **get along**.

figure out
He can't **figure out** the math problem.

run out of
He **ran out of** money.

pay attention to
She's not **paying attention to** the road.

(continued on next page)

run into
She **ran into** a friend.

get rid of
She can't **get rid of** the fly.

look forward to
She's **looking forward to** her vacation.

break down
The car **broke down**.

Vocabulary Practice

Complete the letter with vocabulary words. Use each phrasal verb only once. Use the correct verb form when necessary.

raccoon

July 20

Dear Mom,

Well, we just got back from the worst vacation we've ever had. We started off on the morning of the fifth, and everybody was _____ _____ _____ **1.** a great trip. But pretty soon things started to go wrong. As usual, Brad and Heather fought and fought; you know they don't _____ _____. **2.** Fred got really mad at them. In the afternoon I was driving but I wasn't

_____ _____ _____ **3.** the gas gauge, and pretty soon we _____ _____ _____ gas! After an hour **4.** or so, a woman finally came along and took us to a gas station. In the late afternoon Fred was driving, and just as we were coming into a town the car _____

_____. We took it to a garage and **5.**

they fixed it—it cost a fortune. Then we left for the national park and got there about 8 P.M. It was almost dark, and it took Fred more than an hour to

_____ _____ how to put up **6.** the tent. And he didn't put it up right!

Then, in the middle of the night, we heard noises outside the tent. Some raccoons were stealing our food. They came back every night after that. No matter what we did, we couldn't _____

_____ _____ them. **7.**

The only good thing was that when we were in Florida we _____ _____ **8.** some old friends from college. What a coincidence! It was nice seeing them. I miss you. Write soon.

Love,

Patty

▶ Speaking

Warm up: Talk about the pictures with a partner. • Look at each scene and describe what is happening. • Use **must**, **might**, and **can't** and make guesses about the people.

Then: Create conversations for the people. OR Tell a story. Say as much as you can.

Any idea where Troy is?

Three days later

▶ Writing: A Composition

Write an argument in favor of either guided tours or trips in which you do everything on your own. You might want to begin by telling about a trip that you took and why it was successful or unsuccessful. Use examples to support your argument.

GASOLINE

She's the kind of person who's always there for you.

Receptive Model

Warm up: How often do you need to see your friends in order to keep up your friendship? Listen.

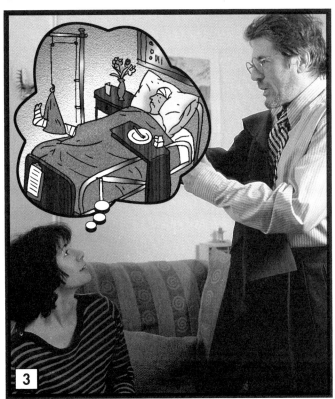

Comprehension: Understanding Meaning from Context

🎧 *Listen to the conversation again. Circle the choice closest in meaning to each underlined word or phrase.*

1. Pat's working, and <u>they're getting by</u>, I guess, but things are pretty tough financially.

    a. they have a lot of money
    b. they have just enough money
    c. they don't have any money at all

2. Yeah, <u>she's a gem</u>.

    a. she's a very smart woman
    b. she's a very good woman
    c. she's a very beautiful woman

3. I'm not <u>thrilled</u> about spending time with Norman, though.

    a. happy
    b. afraid
    c. sad

Listen again. Tell a partner about Pat and Norman. What are they like? What do Dick and Liz think of them? Use your own words. Say as much as you can. 🎧

GRAMMAR AND MEANING

Adjective clauses

Receptive Model

Reading Focus • A Magazine Article

Before You Read: What is your definition of a friend?

Read the article. (Note the examples of adjective clauses in bold type.) 🎧

Friends and Best Friends

by Myra Gormley

My grandmother used to say to me, "You can count the number of your true friends on the fingers of one hand." For a long time I thought this was true. I've discovered that my grandmother was only half right. Maybe we do only make a few "best" friends in our lifetime, but those aren't the only people **that we can call friends**. There are many different types. Let me tell you about a few of them.

One type of friend is the type **that I call the "soccer mom friend."** My neighbor Betty is a good example. We both have kids **who play soccer**, and someone has to take them to their practices and pick them up. Betty and I and two other mothers do this. We meet sometimes and have coffee and talk about what our kids are doing, but those are the only times **that we see each other**. I really enjoy the company of these women, but we don't do anything else together.

Another type is the "hobby friend." This is the person **that you share an interest or a hobby with**. Doug and Charles Fisher, **who are brothers**, are a good example of this type. We all belong to a bird-watching club. Every few weekends the members of the club go on hikes in the wilderness and try to identify different kinds of birds. There's nothing romantic about my relationship with Doug and Charles, of course. We just share an interest in birds.

Then there's the "other half of the couple" type of friend. A man named George Nyberg is a good example. George is married to Carmen, a friend **that I've known since college**. When Carmen married George, I knew that I would have to be George's friend if I wanted to continue to be Carmen's. George and I don't share that many interests, but we do have a friendly relationship. He's part of the package.

Finally, there's the category **that my grandmother was talking about—the true friend or best friend**. I only have two. One is Paul, my husband. The other is Carmen, George's wife. What's a "true" or "best" friend? For me it's the person **that you can talk to for hours**, in a conversation **that goes everywhere and nowhere**. It's also the person **who doesn't try to spare your feelings but tells you the good and the not-so-good things about yourself**.

It would be hard to live without one or two best friends around. But it's good to have the other kinds, too.

Source: Based on information in Judith Viorst's essay, "Friends, Good Friends, and Such Good Friends," where some of these categories are suggested.

Tell your partner about the different kinds of friends Myra Gormley talks about. Use your own words. Say as much as you can.

Adjective Clauses

Adjective clauses give information about nouns or pronouns.

adjective clause

Pat's the kind of person **who is always there for you.**

The adjective clause, **who is always there for you,** describes the noun **person**. It tells what kind of person Pat is.

In adjective clauses, use **that** for things.

I like all my classes, but the one **that I like best** is my physics class.

Use **who** or **that** for people. **Who** is a little more formal than **that**.

Norman is the type of guy **who always has to be right.** (more formal)

Norman is the type of guy **that always has to be right.** (more informal)

GRAMMAR TASK: Find three adjective clauses that describe people in "Friends and Best Friends" on page 98.

Grammar in a Context

Read the conversation. Then complete the last part of the conversation, based on the information. Use adjective clauses.

HOW TO **talk about job possibilities**

Conversation

🎧 *Read and listen to the conversation.*

A: Any interesting jobs?

B: Well, this one sounds like it's right up your alley.

A: Oh?

B: It's for a bilingual secretary. They want someone who speaks French.

A: Great. Is there a fax number? I'll fax them my resume.

🎧 *Listen again and practice.*

Variations

right up your alley
made for you
just what you're looking for

Work with a partner. Talk about job possibilities for you or people you know. Use these ads or bring in ones from a local paper. Use the conversation as a model.

International Job Mart

Lawyer
Attorney with 3–5 years experience in international law. Paris office. Fax resume to 33-1-42-59-98-78.

Artists
Desktop artists
Compose catalog pages. Salary open. Send resume to: 579 Main Street, Suite 100, Doublebay, Sydney, Australia.

College Grad
Leading sports company has several opportunities in New York City. Candidate must have excellent communication skills, 6 months work experience, ability to handle projects from start to finish, good word processing. Call Mr. Bailey: 1-212-757-1111.

Personal Assistant
Assist well-known TV personality. Organize appearances, fan mail. Good typing & MS Word required. Call: 1-310-707-6566.

Multilingual Office Manager
Large international firm based in London seeks Office Manager. Must be fluent in Chinese, English, and one other language. Good word processing skills. Excellent communication skills. High salary. Fax resume to: 44-171-490111.

International Financial Accountant
Degree in accounting or finance. Five years experience. Good salary/ good benefits. Fax: 1-616-909-8907.

☑ **Now you know how to talk about job possibilities.**

HOW TO describe a person's qualities

Conversation

🎧 *Read and listen to the conversation.*

A: What kind of assistant would you prefer?

B: I'd like someone who's well organized.

A: How well organized are you?

B: Well, I'm not that organized myself. That's why I need an assistant who is.

A: What about someone who's punctual?

B: I don't really care one way or the other about that.

🎧 *Listen again and practice.*

Improvise

Read the chart and put checks next to the qualities you see in yourself. Then check qualities that you would like an assistant, a travel companion, a business partner, or a partner for a school project to have. Talk with a partner about the kind of person who would be best for the role. Use the conversation as a model.

Qualities	Me	Person I'm looking for
levelheaded (doesn't get excited easily)	☐	☐
easygoing (doesn't get angry easily)	☐	☐
punctual (always arrives on time)	☐	☐
logical (acts on reasoning, not emotions)	☐	☐
emotional (acts on feelings, not logic)	☐	☐
talkative (talks a lot)	☐	☐
outgoing (is friendly and sociable)	☐	☐
quiet or **reserved** (doesn't talk much)	☐	☐
neat (is clean and orderly)	☐	☐
messy (is not neat)	☐	☐
considerate (thinks of the needs and feelings of others)	☐	☐
industrious (is hardworking)	☐	☐

☑ **Now you know how to describe a person's qualities.**

Authentic Reading

from *Chicken Soup for the Teenage Soul*

Before You Read: *Do you have a best friend? What are some things you like about this person?*

Read this poem by a teenage girl. 🎧

My New Best Friend

Retold by Kimberly Kirberger

Today I met a great new friend
Who knew me right away
It was funny how she understood
All I had to say

She listened to my problems
She listened to my dreams
We talked about love and life
She'd been there, too, it seems

I never once felt judged by her
She knew just how I felt
She seemed to just accept me
And all the problems I'd been dealt

She didn't interrupt me
Or need to have her say
She just listened very patiently
And didn't go away

I wanted her to understand
How much this meant to me
But as I went to hug her
Something startled me

I put my arms in front of me
And went to pull her nearer
And realized that my new best friend
Was nothing but a mirror

Source: *Chicken Soup for the Teenage Soul,* p. 57, Health Communications, Inc.

Comprehension: Inference and Interpretation

Now write some of the qualities the girl who wrote the poem would like in a friend.

Examples: She would like a friend who understands all she has to say.
············ She would like a friend who listens to her problems.

Heart to Heart

Talk with a partner. Compare your opinions.

Talk about the qualities that you wrote down in the Comprehension exercise. Do you think that they are important qualities? Discuss the qualities that you consider most important in a best friend.

 (reinforces adjective clauses)

Partner A's picture

Jack
_____ _____ Jack _____ _____

This is a picture of Jack and four friends: Steve, Cal, Ray, and Peter. Partner B, turn to page 144. Use adjective clauses to tell your partner who the people are. Partner A, write the names under the pictures.

Example: Jack is the one who is wearing the red sweater.

Partner B's picture

Rita
Rita _____ _____ _____ _____

This is a picture of Rita and four friends: Dora, Nina, Lillian, and Stephanie. Partner A, turn to page 143. Use adjective clauses to tell your partner who the people are. Partner B, write the names under the pictures.

Example: Rita is the one who has red hair.

Pronunciation

That

*The word **that** can be stressed /ðǽt/ or unstressed /ðət/.*

🎧 *Listen and repeat.*

1. Thát's an expensive computer.
2. It's a computer that fits in your pocket.
3. It's really not thát difficult to use.
4. Thát guy seems very kind.
5. He's the type of guy that's always there for you.
6. He doesn't live thát far away from you.

🎧 *Now listen to each sentence.*

1. That's the store that has beautiful gifts.
2. That's the one that I want.
3. That clock isn't that expensive and looks very nice.

🎧 *Listen again. Circle each **that** that has stress.*

Listening with a Purpose

Determine Context

🎧 *Listen to the telephone conversation. Then answer the questions. Use your own words.*

1. Who are the speakers? _____

2. Where is Dan? _____

3. What is Dan talking about? _____

Focus Attention

🎧 *Listen to the conversation again. Listen for information about Dan's friends and classes. Then complete each statement by circling the correct letter.*

1. Dan's friend Jim _____.

   a. doesn't study much   **b.** studies an average amount   **c.** studies a lot

2. Dan's friend Jim _____.

   a. goes to bed late   **b.** goes to bed early   **c.** goes to bed at 10 P.M.

3. Dan's friend Tex _____.

   a. doesn't study much   **b.** studies an average amount   **c.** studies a lot

4. Dan's morning English class is _____.

   a. a grammar class   **b.** a writing class   **c.** a literature class

5. Dan's afternoon class is _____.

   a. a writing class   **b.** a grammar class   **c.** a literature class

6. Dan thinks his morning English class is _____.

   a. boring   **b.** interesting   **c.** easy

7. Dan _____ his afternoon English class.

   a. doesn't like   **b.** likes   **c.** loves

Bonus   **Question:** What does Dan mean when he says that it seems like Tex "hardly ever cracks a book"?

_____

In Your Own Words   **Tell a partner about Dan's life at school. Use your own words. Say as much as you can.**

Vocabulary

Relationships

🎧 *Say each word or phrase. Study the definitions.*

a friend: A friend is someone you like and enjoy being with.
> Lauren and I have been **friends** for a long time.

an enemy: An enemy is someone you dislike or hate.
> Ever since Evan and Roger got in a fight, they have been bitter **enemies.**

an acquaintance: An acquaintance is someone you know a little, but not well enough to be friends.
> Mr. Ellis and I are just **acquaintances**—I don't know much about him.

a colleague: A colleague is someone you work with in a professional job.
> My **colleagues** and I go out for lunch every Wednesday.

a relative: A relative is a family member: a cousin, aunt, uncle, grandparent, etc.
> All of Andrea's **relatives** are coming to her house for the holidays.

friendship: Friendship is the relationship between friends.
> My **friendship** with Dawn is very important to me.

close: A close friend is a friend that you know well and like very much.
> My cousin and I grew up together, and we're very **close.**

distant: A distant relationship is one that is not very close.
> Mr. and Mrs. Carr have **a distant** relationship. They never seem happy together.

get mad at: To get mad at someone is to become angry at that person.
> Lorraine **got mad at** John yesterday, and she's still pretty angry.

not speak: When we do not speak to someone, we refuse to talk to that person.
> Lorraine **isn't speaking** to John.

make up: To make up is to become friendly again after being angry.
> I bet Lorraine and John will **make up** tomorrow.

get to know: To get to know someone is to gradually begin to know that person.
> I just met Ellen, but I'd like to **get to know** her better.

Notice that some of these words are opposites.

friends	enemies
close	distant
get mad at	make up

Vocabulary Practice

Look at the pictures. Then complete the statements with vocabulary words.
Use each word or phrase only once. Use the correct form when necessary.

1. These people work together. They are _____.

2. Joan and her _____ are having dinner together.

3. These people are _____.

4. Mrs. Adams is not a close friend; she is just an _____.

5. These people seem to have a _____ relationship.

6. These people have a _____ relationship.

7. The two girls are good _____.

8. The two girls have a close _____.

9. Jack and Susan met a year ago. It didn't take them long to _____ each other.

10. A few months later Susan _____ Jack.

11. After that, Jack and Susan _____ to each other for months.

12. Fortunately, Jack and Susan _____, and now they're close again.

▶ Speaking

Warm up: Talk about the pictures with a partner. • What kind of relationship do the people have in each picture? • How has their relationship changed? • Tell your partner everything you see in the pictures.

Then: Create conversations for the people. OR Tell a story. Say as much as you can.

In Your Own Words

Laura   Adam

15 YEARS LATER

Laura

The Forest Point Times

What kind of _____ would you prefer?

Adam

Any interesting jobs?

Laura   Adam

3 YEARS LATER

▶ Writing: A Composition

Write a composition about a special friendship. Who is the friend? What is special about this person?

Did you think you would live to be a hundred?

Receptive Model

Warm up: Who is the oldest person you know? What have you learned from this person? Read or listen. 🎧

Comprehension: Understanding Meaning from Context

Circle the choice closest in meaning to each underlined word or phrase.

1. I was <u>a real tomboy</u>.

    a. a girl who acted like a boy   **b.** like a boy named Tom   **c.** an honest person

2. People will <u>pay anything to save their skin</u>.

    a. pay a lot of money when they are sick   **b.** pay nothing when they are sick   **c.** spend a little money on their skin

3. I was <u>furious</u> that he never said that to me.

    a. proud   **b.** angry   **c.** delighted

4. I <u>handle stress well</u>.

    a. I often bother people.   **b.** I get angry very easily.   **c.** I don't get too upset when bad things happen.

Tell a partner about Dr. Amelia Breckenridge. Use your own words. Say as much as you can.

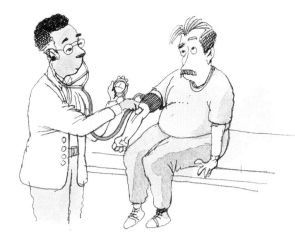

GRAMMAR AND MEANING

Was going to **and** would + base form

Receptive Model

◣ **Listening Focus** • A Conversation

Before You Listen: Is there much stress in your life?
How do you handle stress?

🎧 Listen to the conversation in a doctor's office.

Comprehension: Understanding Grammar from Context

🎧 Listen to the conversation again. Then circle the choice closest in meaning to
each statement from the listening.

1. I was going to get a physical last summer, but then I had to go out of town
on a business trip.

    a. I got a physical.   **b.** I didn't get a physical.   **c.** I probably got a physical.

2. My boss promised he would hire me an assistant, but that hasn't gone
beyond the promise stage yet.

    a. He didn't hire me   **b.** He hired me an assistant.   **c.** I already had an
    an assistant.   assistant.

3. My wife and I were going to spend a week in Europe last spring, but something came up.

    a. We planned to go   **b.** We didn't plan to go to   **c.** We planned to go to
    to Europe, and we   Europe, but we went   Europe, but we
    went.   anyway.   didn't go.

In Your Own Words Jack talks about several problems he has. Tell a partner about some
of Jack's problems. Use your own words. Say as much as you can.

Heart to Heart

Talk with a partner. Compare your opinions.

What things are stressful to you? Is stress always bad,
or can stress add interest and excitement to your life?
Explain.

Was Going to and Would + Base Form

Use **was** (or **were**) **going to** + base form to talk about plans in the past.

<u>was going to</u>   <u>base form</u>
Karen **was going to** **be** a singer like her mother.

Would is the past form of **will**. Use **would** + base form for the same purpose.

<u>would</u>   <u>base form</u>
Karen said she **would** **be** a singer like her mother.

I never thought I**'d become** a doctor.

Amanda said she **would marry** Joshua.

Was going to + base form often suggests that the planned action did not happen. The negative form suggests that it did happen.

We **were going to go** out for dinner last night. (Suggests "but we didn't go.")

Martha **wasn't going to take** a vacation this year. (Suggests "but she took one anyway.")

GRAMMAR TASK: Find an example of **was going to** + base form in the photo story on pages 108–109. Say it again, using **would**.

Grammar in a Context

A. *Complete the conversation. Use the present or the past of* **be going to** *and the indicated verb.*

Did you bring home the pasta and the olive oil?

Oh, I'm sorry. I knew I forgot to do something. I <u>was going to get</u> it
1. get
on my way to work, but traffic was terrible. Then I <u>was going to ask</u>
2. ask
Roger to get it, since he goes out for lunch, but Roger was sick today.

Well, don't worry about it.

I'm glad you're not upset. . . . So, before I forgot the pasta and oil, what <u>were</u> you <u>going to make</u> for dinner?
3. make

Well, I <u>was going to make</u> pasta primavera, but
4. make
now I'<u>m going to make</u> something much better.
5. make

What?

A reservation at Pastina's.

B. *Complete the conversation. Use **would** and the indicated verb or the simple past tense form of the verb.*

How was your physics test?

A piece of cake. I thought it _____ impossible, but
1. be
I _____ all the answers.
2. know

That's great. What _____
you _____ afterwards?
3. do

I _____ to the
4. go
library and studied for
tomorrow's exam.

Well, do you want to wash up for dinner? It'll be ready in a few minutes.

Oh. I didn't think we _____
5. have
dinner so early. I _____ a slice of
6. have
pizza on my way home from the library.

HOW TO **talk about intention**

Conversation

🎧 *Read and listen to the conversation.*

A: Uh-oh.

B: What's wrong?

A: I was going to call my mother as soon as I got here, but I forgot all about it.

B: Call her now.

A: At 11 P.M.?

B: Better late than never. She won't mind.

🎧 *Listen again and practice.*

Improvise

Work with a partner. Look at the notes. Choose one and improvise a conversation.
You have forgotten to do something. Your partner makes a suggestion.
Use the conversation as a model.

Please call Dad as soon as you get home. Ask him to bring home some milk. We're all out.
Love,
Mom

Please call Alice. Ask her to fax me the letter she sent to Dr. Lee

Don't forget to call your brother and wish him a happy birthday.

☑ **Now you know how to talk about intention.**

SOCIAL LANGUAGE 2
How to express concern for someone/empathize

Conversation

🎧 *Read and listen to the conversation.*

A: Are you OK? You look a little frazzled.
B: Oh. It's just the pressure. I'm all stressed out.
A: Why? What's happening?
B: Too much work, too little time.
A: I know just what you mean. You know, maybe you should try yoga.
B: I'm game.

🎧 *Listen again and practice.*

Improvise

Have a conversation with a partner. You are stressed out. Your partner expresses concern and makes a suggestion. Use the conversation as a model.

Some Ideas

try yoga / meditation

take some time off

get a massage

or your OWN idea

join a gym

☑ **Now you know how to express concern for someone. You also know how to empathize.**

SOCIAL LANGUAGE 3

How to cancel a date and apologize/make another date

Conversation

🎧 *Read and listen to the conversation.*

A: See you tomorrow.

B: Oh. I'm sorry. I can't make it.

A: How come? Is everything OK?

B: Yeah, it's just that something came up at work at the last minute. I'm really sorry.

A: How does next week sound?

B: Perfect.

🎧 *Listen again and practice.*

Work with a partner. One of you cancels a date and apologizes. Together, make another arrangement. Use the conversation as a model.

☑ **Now you know how to cancel a date and apologize. You also know how to make another date.**

Receptive Model

Authentic Reading

from *The New York Times*

Before You Read: *At the time this article was written, Jeanne Calment was the world's oldest person, according to official records. What factors cause a person to live a long life?*

Read the article. 🎧

World's oldest person dies in France at age 122

She rode a bicycle until she was 100.

By CRAIG R. WHITNEY

THE NEW YORK TIMES

PARIS—Jeanne Calment, born a year before Alexander Graham Bell patented his telephone and 14 years before Alexandre Gustave Eiffel built his tower, died yesterday in a nursing home in Arles.

At 122, she was the oldest person whose age had been verified by official documents.

Jean-Marie Robine, a public health researcher who is one of the authors of a book about Calment, said she had been in

good health, though almost blind and deaf, as recently as a month ago.

(continued on next page)

The French, who celebrated her as the doyenne of humanity, had their own theories about why she lived so long, noting that she used to eat more than 2 pounds of chocolate a week and treat her skin with olive oil, rode a bicycle until she was 100, and only quit smoking five years ago.

Longevity ran in the family. Calment's mother lived until she was 86 and her father until he was 93. But Robine said her great strength was her unflappability.

"I think she was someone who, constitutionally and biologically speaking, was immune to stress," he said in a telephone interview. "She once said, 'If you can't do anything about it, don't worry about it.'"

She married a cousin, Fernand Nicolas Calment, in 1896. As the prosperous owner of a store in Arles, he was able to support her in style, and she never had to work. She played tennis, took up roller skating, bicycling and swimming, and took great pleasure in joining the hunting parties he organized. She also studied the piano and enjoyed the opera.

Calment rode a bicycle until she was 100, and walked all over Arles to thank those who congratulated her on her birthday that year.

At age 110, her increasing frailty forced her to move into a nursing home.

At the age of 115, she fell and fractured two bones, and her memory began to fail. But she retained a tart wit. "When you're 117, you see if you remember everything!" she once said, rebuking an interviewer five years ago. When somebody took leave by telling her, "Until next year, perhaps," she retorted, "I don't see why not! You don't look so bad to me."

Comprehension: Understanding Meaning from Context

Circle the choice closest in meaning to each underlined word or phrase.

1. Longevity ran in the family.

   a. People in her family were in good health.

   b. People in her family ran to stay healthy.

   c. People in her family lived a long time.

2. I think she was someone who . . . was immune to stress.

   a. was worried about everything

   b. didn't worry about things

   c. couldn't do anything

3. As the prosperous owner of a store in Arles, he was able to support her in style.

   a. successful

   b. poor

   c. only

4. At age 110, her increasing frailty forced her to move into a nursing home.

   a. strength

   b. anger

   c. physical weakness

5. When somebody took leave by telling her, "Until next year, perhaps," she retorted, "I don't see why not! You don't look so bad to me."

   a. answered sadly

   b. answered quickly

   c. repeated

Listening with a Purpose

Focus Attention

🎧 Listen to part of Penelope Goodenough's radio program, "Here's to Your Health."

🎧 Listen to the radio program again. Focus your attention on facts about John. Then complete each statement by circling the correct letter.

1. John works about _____ hours a week.

    a. thirty   **b.** ninety   **c.** seventy

2. John _____ president of his club.

    a. became   **b.** didn't become   **c.** might become

3. John is _____.

    a. divorced   **b.** married   **c.** engaged

4. John is the kind of person who _____.

    a. is always busy   **b.** is seldom busy   **c.** sits quietly and thinks

5. John decided it _____ for him to be lazy.

    a. was OK   **b.** was sometimes OK   **c.** wasn't ever OK

Tell a partner about John's problems. Use your own words. Say as much as you can.

Inter-Action *(reinforces stating an opinion)*

Look at the chart. Rate your city or town. Does a "poor" rating mean that there is more stress? Talk with a partner about the level of stress in your city or town.

	Weather	Air	Water	Jobs	Educational Activities	Hospitals	Control of Crime	Traffic	Transportation	Cultural Activities
Quality										
Excellent *****										
Average * **										
**Poor * **										

ocabulary
Quality of Life

🎧 *Look at the pictures. Say each word or phrase.*

boredom
These teenagers are suffering from **boredom.**

air pollution
Air pollution is a problem here.

water pollution
Water pollution is a problem here.

noise pollution
Noise pollution is a problem here.

standard of living
She has a high **standard of living.**

life expectancy
This animal has a long **life expectancy.**

overcrowded
This area is **overcrowded.**

isolated
This farmhouse is **isolated.**

cope
She can **cope** with stress.

Vocabulary Practice

Complete the following statements with vocabulary words. Use each word or phrase only once.

1. Automobiles and factories are the main causes of _____.

2. When there are too many people in an area, we say the area is _____.

3. Airplanes, loud radios, and car horns are examples of _____.

4. The average time that a person or animal lives is called _____.

5. When people don't have enough to do, they often experience _____.

6. People who don't have any neighbors sometimes feel _____.

7. If you don't get upset when there is a lot of stress, you can _____ with stress.

8. If people live a comfortable life, we often say they have a high _____.

9. Chemicals and garbage in the oceans are examples of _____.

▶ Speaking

Warm up: Talk about the pictures with a partner.
• Compare the two men. Discuss their quality of life. • One of you talks about Alex. The other talks about Todd.

Then: Create conversations for the people. OR Tell a story about a day in the life of one of the men. Say as much as you can.

▶ Writing: A Letter to the Editor

Write a letter to the editor of your local newspaper in which you complain about a problem in your area. What is the problem? What do you want to change?

119

He wants you to call him.
He says it's important.

Warm up: What kinds of things are funny to you? What makes you laugh?
Listen. 🎧

WHILE YOU WERE OUT

_Mr. Byrd_____ .called

will call back	
will stop by	
returned your call	
please call	✓

Number_787-4460_____

Date_____

APRIL 1

APRIL 1

Comprehension: Understanding Meaning from Context

Listen to the conversation again. Circle the choice closest in meaning to each underlined word or phrase.

1. It really <u>dragged</u>. From now on I'm asking people to limit their presentations to five minutes.

    a. went quickly
    b. went slowly
    c. was interesting

2. <u>I'm having trouble getting through.</u>

    a. Someone is already talking on the phone.
    b. I can't hear.
    c. It's too crowded.

3. <u>This is infuriating!</u> I've been trying off and on for the last half hour.

    a. This is wonderful!
    b. This is interesting!
    c. This makes me angry!

4. This is the <u>aviary</u>. How can I help you?

    a. place where birds are kept
    b. place where cats are kept
    c. place where fish are kept

Tell a partner about the joke Laura played on Robert. Why was it funny? Use your own words. Say as much as you can.

Infinitives / verb forms for emphasis

Receptive Model

Reading Focus • A Magazine Article

Before You Read: What are the benefits of laughter?

Read the article. (Note the examples of infinitives and one emphatic verb in bold type.) 🎧

PSYCHOLOGY DIGEST

A Laugh a Minute

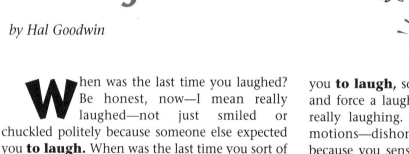

by Hal Goodwin

When was the last time you laughed? Be honest, now—I mean really laughed—not just smiled or chuckled politely because someone else expected you **to laugh.** When was the last time you sort of let yourself go and gave in and giggled until you had tears in your eyes? Been a long time, has it? Let me tell you this: If you're not laughing much, you're missing out on one of the unique human experiences. A sense of humor is one of the qualities that make us human. But what is humor? What are its characteristics?

One aspect of humor is that it seems **to be** based on a violation of expectations. If we see somebody slip on a banana peel and fall, we laugh because normally we don't expect people **to slip** on banana peels. Once at the university I was taking a shower in the dormitory, and my friends stole my clothes. Of course I expected my clothes

to be right outside the shower where I'd left them. My friends thought it would be funny if I had to walk back to my room without my clothes. I had the last laugh, though, because I put the shower curtain on and wore it back to my room. They didn't expect that.

Another aspect of humor is that it usually causes a spontaneous response. Laughter is normally unplanned and uncontrolled. Let's say your friend Linda tells you a joke. You sense that Linda wants

you **to laugh,** so you do. You smile and chuckle and force a laugh **to come out,** but you aren't really laughing. You're just going through the motions—dishonestly. True laughter happens because you sense the humor in a situation and respond pretty much automatically. It doesn't happen because someone else wants you **to laugh.**

One of the most important aspects of humor is that it figures into our overall health. When we allow ourselves **to** really **laugh**, a physiological process happens in our body. Endorphins, hormones that kill pain and contribute to our overall sense of well-being, are manufactured in our brain. Some years ago author Norman Cousins discovered that he was very ill. Doctors told him he had only a

short time **to live.** Refusing **to** just **die,** he asked friends **to tell** him as many funny things as they could. He rented and watched old comedy movies, and he laughed himself silly. His health improved. It's true that Cousins **did die** eventually, but laughter probably helped him **to live** longer than everyone expected.

Do yourself a favor: Monitor yourself for a week and count the number of times you've really laughed. If you find that you haven't had at least one good belly laugh, you're probably taking life too seriously. Go out and rent a Marx Brothers movie.

 **In Your Own Words**

Hal Goodwin says that humor is based on a violation of expectations. What does he mean by "a violation of expectations"? Give your own example. Say as much as you can.

 **Heart to Heart**

Talk with a partner. Compare your opinions.

Reread the third paragraph in the reading. Do you sometimes laugh at a joke that you don't think is funny? Is this dishonest?

Infinitives

An infinitive is **to** + the base form of a verb.

Some verbs can be followed by infinitives: **ask, decide, expect, hope, need, plan, want.**

                infinitive
Mr. Byrd decided **to take** a trip.

Remember that some verbs can be followed by gerunds: **love, like, enjoy, don't care for, dislike, hate, can't stand.**

He enjoys **telling** jokes.

Some verbs can be followed by either an infinitive or a gerund—for example, **like** and **prefer.**

    I like **to laugh.**   I like **laughing.**

To say that someone wants another person to do something, use the following pattern: verb + object + infinitive. (The object must come before the infinitive.)

      verb object infinitive
I **want her to help** me.

These other verbs follow the same pattern: **advise, allow, ask, encourage, expect, force, need, permit, remind, tell, want, would like.**

      verb   object   infinitive
I**'m asking people to limit** their presentations to five minutes.

GRAMMAR TASK: Find an example of the pattern **verb + object + infinitive** in the reading on page 122.

HE WANTS YOU TO CALL HIM. HE SAYS IT'S IMPORTANT.   123

Grammar in a Context 1

Complete the paragraph. Use the correct form of the verb and the infinitive.

A young couple had a four-year-old son. He _____ healthy, but he
1. seem / be

didn't talk. The parents _____ a doctor. The doctor said, "Your son
2. decide / see

_____ lemons." They gave him lemons, but he still didn't speak. They
3. need / eat

went to a speech pathologist. She said, "I _____ with your son every day
4. would like / work

for a month." But, after the month, the boy still didn't speak. Then one morning at

breakfast, the boy said, "Mom, the toast is burned." His mother exclaimed, "You talked! I'm

so happy. But why has it taken so long?"

"Well, up to now," the boy said, "I _____ a thing. Everything was fine."
5. not need / say

Grammar in a Context 2

Dana is leaving for Paris. Read the requests of Dana and her family.
Rewrite each request. Use the verbs in parentheses.

Example: (ask) Dana's mother _asks her to call when she arrives_____.

1. (remind) Her father _____.

2. (ask) Her sister _____.

3. (want) Her brother _____.

4. (tell) Dana _____.

Verb Forms for Emphasis

To emphasize a word, pronounce it with stress. We stress words to insist on something or to contradict something that was said earlier.

A: He's in France.

B: No, he's **not** in France. He's in England.

A: You won't be able to eat all that ice cream.

B: I **will** be able to eat it. I'm very hungry.

To emphasize a verb in the simple present or simple past, use the auxiliaries **do, does,** or **did.** We often include the word **though** in the sentence.

I don't speak French. I **do** speak Italian, *though*.

Do not contract the subject and verb in statements of emphasis.

A: Marsha's not a doctor.

B: Yes, she *is* a doctor. (NOT: ~~Yes, she's a doctor.~~)

GRAMMAR TASK: Find an emphatic verb form in the reading on page 122.

Grammar with a Partner

Work with a partner. First complete the sentences. Read each sentence to your partner. Your partner uses emphatic verbs to contradict you. Then reverse roles.

Example: **A:** You don't like _____jazz_____.

  B: I do like jazz. I go to jazz concerts whenever I can.

1. You don't like _____.
  (name a person or thing)

2. You didn't see _____.
  (name a person or thing and give a time)

3. _____ doesn't have _____.
  (name a person or thing)   (name a thing)

HOW TO give a message

Conversation

🎧 *Read and listen to the conversation.*

A: Any calls for me?

B: A Ted Cranston called.

A: Did he say what he wanted?

B: No, but he asked you to call him back as soon as possible. Here's his number.

A: Thanks. I'll call him right away.

🎧 *Listen again and practice.*

HE WANTS YOU TO CALL HIM. HE SAYS IT'S IMPORTANT. 125

Fill out the message slip for your partner. Then improvise a conversation. Ask whether there were any calls for you. Your partner gives you a message. Use the conversation as a model.

Date _____ Time _____	A.M. ☐ P.M. ☐

WHILE YOU WERE OUT

M _____

Phone _____
Area code · · · · · · · · · · · · Number · · · · · · · · · · · · Extension

TELEPHONED			PLEASE CALL	
WANTS TO SEE YOU			WILL CALL AGAIN	
RETURNED YOUR CALL			URGENT	

☑ **Now you know how to give a message.**

SOCIAL LANGUAGE 2

HOW TO **express strong agreement**

Conversation

🎧 *Read and listen to the conversation.*

A: That Liz is funny.
B: I'll say. I think she should be a comedian.
A: Really?
B: I'm serious. I really do think she'd be a great comedian.
A: Why don't you tell her?
B: Maybe I will.

🎧 *Listen again and practice.*

Variations

I'll say.
You said it.
That's an understatement.

Work with a partner. Talk about a third person's talents or abilities and what you think the person should do with them. Use the conversation as a model.

Some Ideas

- funny / a comedian
- artistic / a painter
- good at ice-skating / a hockey player
- good at singing / an opera singer or a rock singer
- cooks well / a caterer or a restaurant owner
- speaks French well / a French teacher

or your OWN idea

☑ **Now you know how to express strong agreement.**

HOW TO **ask for a promise/agree to a promise**

Conversation

🎧 *Read and listen to the conversation.*

A: I'm sorry. Are you still angry?

B: No. . . . Just promise me you'll never play a practical joke on me again.

A: I give you my word.

B: Thanks.

🎧 *Listen again and practice.*

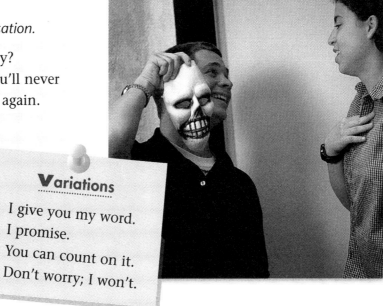

Variations

I give you my word.
I promise.
You can count on it.
Don't worry; I won't.

Improvise a conversation with a partner. Your partner did something you didn't like and apologizes. Accept the apology but ask your partner not to do it again. Use the conversation as a model.

Some Ideas

- call me "honey"
- read my e-mail / mail
- listen to my voice mail
- borrow my clothes / car
- laugh at my mistakes

or your OWN idea

☑ **Now you know how to ask for and agree to a promise.**

Inter-Action *(practices telling a story)*

Work with a partner.

Partner A, turn to page 143. Partner B, turn to page 144.

Read the start of each of your three jokes. Your partner will read the endings. Together, decide on the correct ending for each joke.

Authentic Reading

from *Reader's Digest*

Before You Read: Do you enjoy telling jokes? Is it easy for you to remember jokes that you hear?

Work with a partner. Partner A, read your joke. Practice telling it. Then close your book. Tell the joke to your partner. Then, Partner B, do the same with your joke.

Partner A

IN A PANIC, a traveler called down to the hotel's front desk soon after checking in. "Help!" he yelled. "I'm trapped inside my room."

"What do you mean, trapped?"

"Well, I see three doors," the man explained. "The first opens to a closet, and the second to a bathroom. And the third door has a 'Do Not Disturb' sign hanging on it."

–Peter S. Greenberg

Partner B

"WHEN I WAS A YOUNGSTER," complained the frustrated father, "I was disciplined by being sent to my room without supper. But my son has his own color TV, phone, computer, and CD player."

"So what do you do?" asked his friend.

"I send him to my room!"

Talk with your partner. Which joke do you prefer? What makes the jokes funny? Say as much as you can.

Listening with a Purpose

Focus Attention

Listen to the conversation between a husband and wife.

*Listen to the conversation again for the facts. Then mark each statement **true** or **false**.*

		True	False
1.	Robert had a hard time making his call.	☐	☐
2.	Robert got mad when Laura and Catherine played a joke on him at work.	☐	☐
3.	Greg and Marsha are coming for dinner.	☐	☐
4.	Robert forgot to pick up the steaks.	☐	☐
5.	Allison played a joke on Robert.	☐	☐

Listening Between the Lines

🎧 *Now listen between the lines to predict what will happen next. Tell a partner your prediction.*

Pronunciation
Stress for Contradiction

🎧 *Listen.*

A: You didn't like my party.

B: I <u>did</u> like your party.

A: You can't play the guitar.

B: I <u>can</u> play the guitar.

Now work with a partner. Partner A, read your sentences. Partner B, contradict Partner A. Use stress to make your answer stronger. Then reverse roles.

Partner A's Sentences

1. You can speak Russian.
2. You're not interested.
3. You don't understand that joke.

Partner B's Sentences

1. You can't touch your toes.
2. You heard that joke.
3. You told him my secret.

Vocabulary
Participial Adjectives

🎧 *Look at the pictures. Say each word.*

disappointing
The situation is **disappointing.**
The man is **disappointed.**

relaxing
The beach is **relaxing.**
The people are **relaxed.**

embarrassing
The situation is **embarrassing.**
The man is **embarrassed.**

interesting
The book is **interesting.**
The man is **interested.**

exciting
The show is **exciting.**
The audience is **excited.**

frightening
The dog is **frightening.**
The man is **frightened.**

entertaining
The show is **entertaining.**
The audience is **entertained.**

boring
The TV show is **boring.**
The woman is **bored.**

Vocabulary Practice

Choose the correct words to complete the letter.

August 10

Dear Mom and Dad,

Nadia and I are having a great time in England. We spent Monday, Tuesday, and Wednesday

touring London. For me the most _____ place was the Tower of London—you
1. interesting / interested

know how much I like history. We were there all morning. I wanted to stay longer, but Nadia

was _____, so we left and went to Buckingham Palace.
2. boring / bored

A really funny thing happened on Tuesday morning at our bed and breakfast. I was already

down at breakfast, and Nadia was still taking a shower. She didn't have any clothes with her; all

she had was a towel. Well, she got locked in the bathroom. The owner had to call a locksmith.

When he finally got the door open, Nadia was really _____. Everyone else
3. embarrassing / embarrassed

thought the whole situation was pretty funny, though.

Tuesday night we went to a play in the theater district. It was a comedy—very

_____. On Wednesday, we were on the underground when the train got stuck
4. entertaining / entertained

in the tunnel. It took two hours for them to get the train started, and we were both a little

_____ for a while because the air was getting pretty bad. Because of that, we
5. frightening / frightened

missed a concert in Green Park. We were really _____.
6. disappointing / disappointed

On Thursday we went to Brighton. Or at least we thought we were going to Brighton.

It turned out that we were on a train going north, not south. We met this really nice man who

looked just like Elvis Presley. Nadia was convinced it was him, but of course it wasn't. We had a

great conversation on the train.

Well, tonight at 11 P.M. we're taking the train through the Chunnel to Paris. I don't think it's

going to be a _____ trip, but I don't care. I'm really _____ about
7. relaxing / relaxed   **8. exciting / excited**

seeing Paris.

Love,

Jane

► **Speaking**

Warm up: Talk about the picture with a partner. • Describe the people—for example, "The boy in the red baseball cap looks bored." • Talk about what people think about the fair—for example, "The children think the magician is exciting."

Then: Create conversations for the people. OR Tell a story about the day at the fair. Say as much as you can.

In Your Own Words

I'm sorry.

► **Writing:** A True Story

Write about a funny incident that happened to you at some time in your life. Why was it funny? Was there anyone who did not think it was funny?

131

Review, SelfTest, and Extra Practice

Part 1

Review

That's Way Over My Budget!

🎧 Listen to the conversation.

6

SelfTest

Comprehension: Factual Recall

🎧 *Listen to the conversation again. Then complete each sentence by circling the correct letter.*

1. The car that the woman wants to buy costs about _____.
   a. two thousand dollars   **b.** four thousand dollars   **c.** eight thousand dollars

2. The car that her friend wants her to buy costs about _____.
   a. two thousand dollars   **b.** four thousand dollars   **c.** eight thousand dollars

3. The salesman says the car that the woman wants was owned by a _____.
   a. teacher   **b.** doctor   **c.** mechanic

4. The car that the woman wants is _____.
   a. five years old   **b.** two years old   **c.** four years old

5. The woman doesn't buy the blue car because _____.
   a. she doesn't like the car   **b.** it costs too much   **c.** she doesn't like the color blue

6. The car that the woman buys is _____.
   a. in excellent condition   **b.** in OK condition   **c.** not in very good condition

Comprehension: Grammar Review

🎧 *Listen to the conversation again. Then complete the following sentences with the correct words.*

1. I can't believe it. There _____ _____ something wrong with it. That's too cheap.

2. It was owned by an elderly lady _____ _____ a teacher.

3. Well, there's got to be something wrong with this car. I just don't know _____

   _____ _____.

4. Oh, no. I'm sorry. But remember: I _____ _____ _____ _____

   _____ it.

5. I was pretty sure something like this _____ _____ _____ _____.

Talk with a partner. Compare your opinions.

Think about the conversation on pages 132–133. Which of the following proverbs best describes what this story is about?

   a. Dirty hands make clean money.

   b. A new day, a new dollar.

   c. You get what you pay for.

What does the man mean when he says, "It was just too good to be true"? Is the price of something a good indication of its quality?

Grammar with a Partner

Talk with a partner.

If two friends were coming to your city or town,

   1. What would you advise them to do or not to do?

   2. Where would you encourage them to stay? How long would you encourage them to stay?

   3. What would you tell them to bring?

   4. What would you remind them to do before leaving?

   5. Would you give them any other suggestions or information about your town?

Part 2

Review

Authentic Reading:

from *And More by Andy Rooney*

Before You Read: *Do you think that most people agree about what is beautiful? Do you think that people who work quickly usually do a good job?*

Here are excerpts from an essay by Andy Rooney. Read what he thinks about some North American proverbs.

Proverbs for the New Year

This year I got to thinking that some of those old sayings aren't true.

Take, for example, the saying "Beauty is in the eye of the beholder."

I happen to think that this is not true at all. Some things are beautiful and some are not. If you don't know which is which, that's your shortcoming, or mine, but the quality of the object is unchanged. We always have different experiences that influence our attitude toward something, but the fact is that the world's most knowledgeable art experts would not disagree very much on which are the best paintings. You can say "Beauty is in the eye of the beholder" or you can say "That's your opinion," but once two people know all about a subject, they almost always agree. We disagree on things when one person knows more than the other.

"Haste makes waste." Baloney. Haste usually saves time. Most of us move too slowly. The fastest workers are the people who know how to do the job best. I can fuss with a little job of carpentry for days, but if we get a professional carpenter in to make some china closets in the dining room, he's finished before I'd have figured out where to put them. Haste only makes waste if you don't know what you're doing.

Reprinted with the permission of Scribner, a division of Simon & Schuster from *And More by Andy Rooney* by Andrew A. Rooney. Copyright © 1982 Essay Productions, Inc.

SelfTest

Comprehension: Understanding Meaning from Context

Circle the choice closest in meaning to each underlined word or phrase.

1. Beauty is in the eye of the beholder.

  a. person who is looking at the item

  b. person who is beautiful

  c. person who is near the item

2. Haste makes waste.

  a. You shouldn't throw things in the garbage.

  b. You shouldn't spend your money.

  c. You shouldn't do things too fast.

3. Baloney. Haste usually saves time.

  a. I agree.

  b. I disagree.

  c. It's all the same to me.

4. I can fuss with a little job of carpentry for days.

  a. spend a lot of time on

  b. do a great job on

  c. do a terrible job on

Comprehension: Inference and Interpretation

Read the statements. Put a check next to the sentences that are true, according to Andy Rooney.

1. ☐ Experts usually agree on what is beautiful.

2. ☐ The same thing can be beautiful and ugly. It all depends on who is looking at it.

3. ☐ People who work quickly usually do so because they know what they're doing.

4. ☐ Doing things quickly actually takes longer.

Heart to Heart

Talk with a partner. Discuss the proverbs "Beauty is in the eye of the beholder" and "Haste makes waste." Compare your opinions.

Do you agree with Rooney? Why or why not? Do you know any other proverbs about beauty or about working quickly? What are they?

Writing

Choose one of these proverbs and write a composition about why you agree or disagree with it. Give examples to support your opinion.

Beauty is in the eye of the beholder.
Haste makes waste.
You get what you pay for.

Part 3

Review

Advertisements

🎧 *Listen to the advertisements.*

Fantastic Fences

Miller's Kids' Clothes

Timely Transportation

GREAT GARDENS

SelfTest

Comprehension: Confirming Content

🎧 *Listen to the advertisements again. Match each ad with the correct product or service.*

Ad number 1 is for _____.   fences

Ad number 2 is for _____.   transportation

Ad number 3 is for _____.   gardening services

Ad number 4 is for _____.   children's clothes

Comprehension: Factual Recall

🎧 *Now listen once more and look at the pictures. Write the name of the company offering each product or service.*

Ad number 1   _____

Ad number 2   _____

Ad number 3   _____

Ad number 4   _____

Look at the pictures. Think about the meaning of each proverb.

Good fences make good neighbors.

Better three hours too soon than one minute too late.

The grass is always greener on the other side of the fence.

The clothes make the man.

Talk with a partner about the meaning of each proverb. Do you agree or disagree?

Now listen again to the four advertisements on page 137. Match each advertisement with one of the proverbs. Explain your reasoning.

Ad number 1 _____

Ad number 2 _____

Ad number 3 _____

Ad number 4 _____

SOCIAL LANGUAGE Review

Review 1

🎧 *Read and listen to the conversation.*

A: Any calls while I was out?

B: A Will Casperson called.

A: Will? You must be kidding. I haven't seen him for a while.

B: Who is he?

A: He's my friend who lives in the country—in West Lakewood.

B: That's pretty far away.

A: I'll say. . . .You see that painting over there?

B: Yeah.

A: Well, Will did it.

B: It's pretty good. Is he a professional painter?

A: No, he only paints from time to time.

B: What does he do?

A: He actually does a lot of things, but he's never found anything he's stayed with. Will is what we call "a jack-of-all-trades and master of none."

Improvise

Work with a partner. Your partner tells you about a call that came for you while you were out. Tell your partner about the person who called. Use the conversation as a model.

Review 2

🎧 *Read and listen to the conversation.*

A: Any idea where Jill is?

B: At the moment she might be over Iceland.

A: Over Iceland?

B: Yeah. She's on her way to Europe.

A: Oh?

B: I was going to tell you yesterday, but I forgot. She has a meeting in Paris tomorrow. She'll probably be out for three days.

A: Now that I think of it, she mentioned something about a meeting in Paris this month. That Jill really gets around. She was in Tokyo and Seoul last week, and next month she's going to Rio. When does she ever sleep?

B: I think Jill believes the less you sleep, the more you get out of life.

A: I think you're right.

Improvise a conversation with a partner. One of you asks where someone else is. Make guesses about where the person is and talk about that person. Use the conversation as a model.

SOCIAL LANGUAGE SelfTest

Circle the appropriate statement or question to complete each of the following conversations.

1. **A:** Do you need a ride home?

   B: _____

   a. Yes. I have no idea what to take.

   b. Yes. It's no trouble.

   c. Yes. I'd appreciate it.

2. **A:** Guess where I'm going.

   B: _____

   a. You must be kidding.

   b. I give up.

   c. I can't wait.

3. **A:** _____

   B: I don't care one way or the other.

   a. Was she a good typist?

   b. Do you want someone who's a good typist?

   c. Are you a typist?

4. **A:** You look a little frazzled.

   B: _____

   a. Try yoga.

   b. When did it happen? I heard about it.

   c. I know. It's all the pressure.

5. A: That Sue is smart.

   B: _____

      a. I'll say.

      b. When?

      c. Where is that?

6. A: Promise me you won't do that again.

   B: _____

      a. I'll say.

      b. Don't worry; I won't.

      c. I know what you mean.

7. A: _____

   B: She's a biology professor.

      a. Do you know what she does?

      b. You mean the woman over there?

      c. No wonder she knows so much about science.

8. A: Any idea where Sheila is?

   B: _____

      a. She might work hard.

      b. She might go to work.

      c. She might be at work.

9. A: What kind of person are you looking for?

   B: _____

      a. I'm looking.

      b. Someone who's well organized.

      c. Who's well organized?

10. A: _____

   B: How come? Is everything OK?

      a. Sorry, but I can't go to the movies tomorrow.

      b. You look really stressed.

      c. Uh-oh.

Activity Links

Inter-Action

Partner A

Read about your video. Answer your partner's questions.

Cinema Paradiso

Cinema Paradiso follows the life of Salvatore, a boy in a small Italian village. During his free time, Salvatore visits the movies at the Cinema Paradiso. He is enchanted by the movies, and he longs to know the secret of the cinema's magic. Alfredo, the projectionist, agrees to teach the mysteries of movie making to him. As the years pass, Salvatore and Alfredo become great friends.

When Salvatore is old enough to leave the village and pursue a filmmaking career, Alfredo makes him promise never to look back, to always move forward. Salvatore keeps his promise for thirty years until one day a message arrives from his village, calling him back home, where he discovers a wonderful secret.

Director: Giuseppe Tornatore;
Alfredo: Philippe Noiret; **Salvatore (adult):** Jacques Perrin;
Salvatore (child): Salvatore Cascio;
Salvatore (adolescent): Marco Leonardi;
Elena (adolescent): Agnese Nano; **Elena (adult):** Brigitte Fossey;
Producers: Mino Barbera, Franco Cristaldi, Giovanna Romagnoli;
Year: 1988; **Label:** Tartan Video TVL1109;
Length: 117 min; **Cert:** PG;
Sound credit: Hi-Fi Stereo

Unit 2

Game

Answers to Team A's questions:	Answers to Team B's questions:
1. b	1. a
2. c	2. c
3. a	3. c
4. a	4. b
5. c	5. b
6. a	6. c
7. b	7. b

Unit 7

Game

Note: The following lists of answers using *might* include some, but not all, possible answers.

Answers: 2. Germany, Austria, Hungary, Czech Republic, Slovakia, Yugoslavia, Romania, Bulgaria (might); 3. Hungary (must); 5. Italy, Switzerland, Corsica, France, Malta, Eritrea, Somalia, Libya, Ethiopia, countries in North and South America (might); 6. Switzerland (must); 8. United States, Canada, Australia, New Zealand, Bahamas, Barbados, Belize, Bermuda, Brunei, Fiji, Guyana, Hong Kong, Jamaica, Liberia, Malaysia, Singapore, Trinidad and Tobago (might); 9. Australia (must); 12. Egypt, Mexico, Guatemala, China, Spain, Honduras, El Salvador, Belize, Peru (might); 13. Mexico (must); 15. Russia, Serb Republic, Belorussia, Bulgaria, Czech Republic, Slovakia, Poland, Croatia, Slovenia, Ukraine (might); 16. Russia (must); 18. Kenya, Uganda, Tanzania, Zanzibar, Comoro Islands, Congo (might); 19. Tanzania (must)

Unit 8

Inter-Action

Partner A

Use adjective clauses to tell your partner who the people in the picture are.

Rita   Dora   Lillian   Nina   Stephanie

Unit 10

Inter-Action

Partner A

Partner A's jokes:

1. Gracie Allen's electric clock didn't work. She called a repairman and asked him to fix her clock. The repairman checked the clock and said, "There's nothing wrong with the clock. You didn't have it plugged in." Gracie replied, "_____."

2. A teacher asked a little girl to tell her the name of the little girl's new brother. The little girl replied, "_____."

3. The zoo built a special 8-foot-high enclosure for its newly acquired kangaroo, but the next morning the animal was found hopping around outside. The height of the fence was increased to 15 feet, but the kangaroo got out again. Exasperated, the zoo director had the height increased to 30 feet, but the kangaroo still escaped. A giraffe asked the kangaroo, "How high do you think they'll build the fence?" The kangaroo replied, "_____."

Endings for Partner B's jokes:

a. "Well, the way you are going, it's about 24,996 miles, but if you turn around, it's about 4."

b. "I just don't know when to stop."

c. "Who, me?"

ACTIVITY LINKS   143

Inter-Action

Partner B

Read about your video. Answer your partner's questions.

Chariots of Fire

Chariots of Fire is the exciting true story of Harold Abrahams and Eric Liddell, two champion British runners who won gold medals at the 1924 Olympics. Abrahams, a driven Jewish Cambridge student, pursues athletic victory as a way of proving himself and rising above prejudice. Liddell, a devout Scottish missionary, runs to glorify his god.

At the Olympic games, held in France, Abrahams finally achieves complete focus and wins his race. Liddell, holding to his religious beliefs, refuses to run his major event, scheduled on a Sunday, but after a teammate offers to switch events with him, he wins a gold medal and a legendary victory for Britain.

Chariots of Fire, one of the best pictures of the decade, won four Academy Awards in 1982, including Best Picture.

The Cast

Ben Cross	Harold Abrahams
Ian Charleson	Eric Liddell
Nigel Havers	Lord Andrew Lindsay
Ian Holm	Coach Mussabini
Sir John Gielgud	Master of Trinity
Lindsay Anderson	Master of Caius
David Yelland	Prince of Wales
Nicholas Farrell	Aubrey Montague

Some Credits

Directed by	Hugh Hudson
Produced by	David Puttnam
Screenplay by	Colin Welland

Runtime:
    UK:123
Cinematography:
    David Watkin
Music:
    Vangelis
U.S. Distributor:
    Warner Brothers

Inter-Action

Partner B

Use adjective clauses to tell your partner who the people in the picture are.

Ray   Steve   Jack   Cal   Peter

Unit 10

Inter-Action

Partner B

Partner B's jokes:

1. A tourist stopped his car on a country road and asked a young boy to tell him how far it was to Smithville. The boy said, "_____."

2. A grammar teacher pointed to a student and said, "I want you to name two pronouns." The student looked up and said, "_____."

3. After a spelling test, a young boy said to his friend, "I *do* know how to spell 'banana'. _____."

Endings for Partner A's jokes:

a. I don't know yet. We can't understand a word he says.

b. I don't know. Maybe 1,000 feet if they continue to leave the gate unlocked.

c. I don't want to waste electricity, so I only plug it in when I want to know what time it is.

Appendices

Key Vocabulary

This list represents key words and expressions presented in Book 3.

Unit 1

Nouns

Movies and theaters

audience
balcony
cast
center aisle
curtain
left aisle
lobby
movie review
orchestra

popcorn
program
refreshment stand
right aisle
screen
special effects
stage
subtitles
usher

Verbs

be stuck in traffic
move over

Adverb

part-time

Expressions

To ask someone to repeat

Excuse me?
Sorry?
What did you say?
What was that?

To make polite requests

Could you please...?
Would you mind...?

Other expressions

(It's) supposed to be (adjective).
keep an eye on (something)
No problem.
Not at all.

Unit 2

Nouns

News and other media

edition
editor
editorial
media
news
news story
newspaper
protest
publisher
reporter

Other nouns

conflict
permit
video games

Verbs

conflict
cover
object
park
permit
print
protest
run

Adjective

educational

Expressions

To ask about rules

Are you allowed to...?
Are you sure?

To express certainty

Absolutely.
I'm absolutely sure.
I'm certain.
I'm positive.
I'm sure.

To ask about an opinion

Do you think...?
How do you feel about...?
What do you mean?

To express an opinion

I'm all for (something).
It depends.
Not at all.

Unit 3

Nouns

Food and restaurants

appetizer
atmosphere
course
entrée
fast food
junk food
location
meal
reservation
service
tip

Occupations and businesses

catering business
financial advisor
full-time mom / dad
graphic designer
magician
restaurant manager

Verbs

eat out
gain weight
get into (something)
go out to eat
lose weight

Modals

may *(present or future possibility)*
might *(present or future possibility)*

Adjectives

To describe food and restaurants

Indian
lousy
nutritious
out of this world
so-so

Tag questions

...aren't you?
...did you?
...don't you?
...have you?

Expressions

Boy, was I surprised!
One thing leads to another.
Wow, what a day.
You can't miss it.
you guys

Unit 4

Nouns

Places of residence

apartment complex
town house

Building materials

brick
stone
stucco
wood

Parts of a house

attic
back door
basement
deck
front door
garage
garden
gate
porch
roof
stairway

Other nouns

crime
cultural activities
factories
pollution
smog

Verbs

plan ahead
quit (a job)

Adjectives

broke
convenient
crowded

Adverbs

downstairs
easily
far
(work) hard
just
upstairs

Expressions

*To make comparisons
of equality*

as + adj / adv + as
as many + count noun
+ as
as much + noncount
noun + as
not (+ verb) as many +
count noun + as
not (+ verb) as much +
noncount noun
+ as
not as + adj / adv + as

*To emphasize an
opinion*

absolutely
Believe me.
I can't believe it.
I really think...
If you ask me...
In my opinion...
It seems to me...
Take it from me.
Take my word for it.

Other expressions

I guess so.
need a change
used to + base form of
verb
Why in the world...?

Unit 5

Nouns

Honesty and dishonesty

lie
truth
white lie

Verbs

Honesty and dishonesty

lie
tell the truth
trust

Other verbs

cheer (someone) up
let (someone) know
lose (a job)
make an excuse
regret
take a drive

Modals

For possibility

could
might
would

Adjectives

Honesty and dishonesty

dishonest
honest

Other adjectives

blue
down
down in the dumps
miserable

Expressions

*To persuade someone
not to act impulsively*

Calm down.
Relax.
Take it easy.

Other expressions

Finders keepers, losers
weepers.
I've had it.
mind one's own
business
Satisfaction guaranteed
Sounds too good to be
true.
What's the problem?

Unit 6

Nouns

Polite and impolite

behavior
body language
personal space
privacy
territory

Other nouns

autograph
lift
movie director

Verbs

Polite and impolite

(I can) manage
belong
gesture
invade

Adjective

rude

Conjunctions

if
whether

Expressions

To offer an explanation

no wonder
now I understand why
that explains why

*To offer and accept /
decline help*

I can manage
I'd appreciate it.
If that's the case...
It's nice of you to offer.
It's no trouble at all.

Other expressions

I have no idea
I wonder
I'm pretty sure
I've got to run
whether or not

Unit 7

Nouns

Travel and adventure

birth certificate
guided tour
naturalization
    certificate

Modals

To state conclusions

can't

might
must

*To show obligation or
    advisability*

must
should

Phrasal verbs

break down
figure out
get along

get rid of
look forward to
pay attention to
run into
run out of

Adjective

valid

Expressions

To express surprise

At this hour?
You can't be serious.
You can't mean that.
You must be joking.
You must be kidding.

Other expressions

Any idea...?
I can't wait.
I give up.

Unit 8

Nouns

Relationships

acquaintance
colleague
enemy
friend
friendship
relative

Verbs

Relationships

get mad at
get to know
make up
not speak

Adjectives

Relationships

close
distant

Other adjectives

bilingual
organized
punctual

Expressions

*To talk about job
    possibilities*

just what you're
    looking for
made for you
right up your alley

Other expression

I don't care one way
    or the other.

Unit 9

Nouns

Quality of life

air pollution
boredom
life expectancy
noise pollution
standard of living
water pollution

Verb

cope

Adjectives

Quality of life

isolated
overcrowded

Other adjective

frazzled

Expressions

*To talk about plans or
    to indicate
    willingness*

was / were going to +
    base form
would + base form

*To make a suggestion
    to relieve stress*

get a massage
join a gym

take some time off
try yoga / meditation

Other expressions

a piece of cake
Better late than
    never.
How come?
I can't make it.
I'm game.
Something came up.
stressed out

Unit 10

Nouns

Professions

comedian
hockey player
opera singer
painter
restaurant owner
rock singer

Other nouns

joke
practical joke

voice mail

Adjectives

Participial adjectives

boring / bored
disappointing /
    disappointed
embarrassing /
    embarrassed
entertaining /
    entertained
exciting / excited
frightening /
    frightened

interesting /
    interested
relaxing / relaxed

Other adjectives

artistic
funny

Expressions

*To express strong
    agreement*

I'll say.
That's an
    understatement.
You said it.

To agree to a promise

Don't worry; I won't.
I give you my word.
I promise.
You can count on it.

Common Irregular Verbs

The following list is provided for reference. Not all of these verbs appear in *True Colors*.

Base Form	Simple Past	Past Participle
be	was, were	been
beat	beat	beaten
become	became	become
begin	began	begun
bend	bent	bent
bet	bet	bet
bite	bit	bitten
blow	blew	blown
break	broke	broken
bring	brought	brought
build	built	built
buy	bought	bought
*can	could	been able to
catch	caught	caught
choose	chose	chosen
come	came	come
cost	cost	cost
cut	cut	cut
deal	dealt	dealt
dig	dug	dug
do	did	done
draw	drew	drawn
drink	drank	drunk
drive	drove	driven
eat	ate	eaten
fall	fell	fallen
feed	fed	fed
feel	felt	felt
fight	fought	fought
fit	fit, fitted	fit, fitted
fly	flew	flown
forget	forgot	forgotten
forgive	forgave	forgiven
freeze	froze	frozen
get	got	gotten
give	gave	given
go	went	gone
grind	ground	ground
grow	grew	grown
hang	hung, hanged	hung, hanged
have	had	had
hear	heard	heard
hide	hid	hidden
hit	hit	hit
hold	held	held
hurt	hurt	hurt
keep	kept	kept
know	knew	known
lead	led	led
leave	left	left
lend	lent	lent
let	let	let

* *Can* is a modal.

Base Form	Simple Past	Past Participle
light	lit, lighted	lit, lighted
lose	lost	lost
make	made	made
mean	meant	meant
meet	met	met
*must	had to	had to
put	put	put
quit	quit	quit
read	read	read
ride	rode	ridden
ring	rang	rung
rise	rose	risen
run	ran	run
say	said	said
see	saw	seen
sell	sold	sold
send	sent	sent
set	set	set
sing	sang	sung
shake	shook	shaken
shoot	shot	shot
show	showed	shown
shrink	shrank	shrunk
shut	shut	shut
sit	sat	sat
sleep	slept	slept
slide	slid	slid
speak	spoke	spoken
speed	sped	sped
spend	spent	spent
spread	spread	spread
stand	stood	stood
steal	stole	stolen
stick	stuck	stuck
sting	stung	stung
strike	struck	struck
swear	swore	sworn
sweep	swept	swept
swim	swam	swum
swing	swung	swung
take	took	taken
teach	taught	taught
tear	tore	torn
tell	told	told
think	thought	thought
throw	threw	thrown
understand	understood	understood
wake	woke	woken
wear	wore	worn
win	won	won
wind	wound	wound
write	wrote	written

* *Must* is a modal.

Adjectives and Adverbs

Regular

Adjective	Adverb
actual	actually
bad	badly
careful	carefully
careless	carelessly
clear	clearly
easy	easily
fortunate	fortunately
general	generally
happy	happily
normal	normally
quick	quickly
rapid	rapidly
real	really
sincere	sincerely
slow	slowly
true	truly
usual	usually

Irregular

Adjective	Adverb
early	early
fast	fast
good	well
hard	hard

Grammatical Terms

present continuous	I**'m making** dinner right now.
simple present tense	Eric **likes** hamburgers.
past tense of *be*	I **was** at work yesterday.
simple past tense	We **played** soccer last weekend.
habitual past (no longer true)	I **used to play** tennis, but I don't anymore.
past continuous	I **was sleeping** when the phone rang.
present perfect	I**'ve had** the flu for three days.
present perfect continuous	Karen **has been looking** for you.
real conditional	**If** I **have** time, I**'ll visit** you.
present unreal conditional	**If** I **had** a car, I **wouldn't take** the bus to work.
the future with *be going to*	We**'re going to see** a play tonight.
the future with *have to*	Alice **has to work** tomorrow.
the future with the present continuous	I**'m studying** tomorrow.
the future with *will*	Sam **will arrive** next week.
infinitive	I want **to go** home.
gerund	Alex hates **driving**.
noun	That **restaurant** has great **food**.
verb	Sheila **runs** five miles a day.
adjective	That's a **beautiful** hat.
adverb	Amber speaks **quietly**.
present participle	Don is **reading** that book.
past participle	I haven't **seen** that movie yet.

The Passive Voice

Passive Voice

This class **is taught** by Ms. Davis.
"The Moonlight Sonata" **was composed** by Beethoven.
Lunch **will be served** at 1:00.

(Active Voice)

Ms. Davis **teaches** this class.